It's UpHill
Most of the
Way Down

Lynn and Clare,

appreciate having
you as neighbors.
Enjoy the book. Hope
it brings you hope
and encouragement.

God bless,
Barry Jane

A Journey of Adventure and Faith

It's UpHill
Most of the
Way Down

Dr. Barry L. Lane & Jodi L. Raisl

TATE PUBLISHING & Enterprises

Published by Tate Publishing & Enterprises, LLC
127 E. Trade Center Terrace | Mustang, Oklahoma 73064 USA
1.888.361.9473 | www.tatepublishing.com

Tate Publishing is committed to excellence in the publishing industry. The company reflects the philosophy established by the founders, based on Psalm 68:11,
"The Lord gave the word and great was the company of those who published it."

Book design copyright © 2008 by Tate Publishing, LLC. All rights reserved.
Cover design by Joey Garrett
Interior design by Kandi Evans

Published in the United States of America

ISBN:978-1-60604-775-0
1.biography & Autobiography / Adventurers & Explorers
2. Biography & Autobiography / Personal Memoirs
09.12.19

Acknowledgements

I am keenly aware that many people contributed to my safety and learning curve during the course of this epic adventure. This book is as much their legacy as it is my own. I will forever appreciate trip sponsor Vern Schield for providing me this opportunity, and my numerous travel companions for their humor, hard work, knowledge, and courage as we tested ourselves and our faith against the wiles of nature and weather for five full months.

My entire family deserves acknowledgement for their support and feedback as I embraced the challenge of capturing this portion of my life story in a book that might bring joy, inspiration, and encouragement to readers engaged in their own journey of adventure and faith. At some point, most members of my immediate family were asked to read, help edit, or comment on a section of the book. Their candid insights, questions, and comments were sometimes humbling, but always valuable.

Special recognition needs to be given to my daughter, Jodi, who provided the primary impetus to capture this story in book form. She spent countless hours word processing, editing, writing content based on my journal notes, and providing me with feedback on the book's overall layout and the readability of each chapter. She also managed all the complex details related to finding an appropriate publisher. Her drive kept this project moving forward.

A heartfelt expression of gratitude to all that have made writing *It's Uphill Most of the Way Down* another successful journey in my life.

–Dr. Barry L. Lane

S pecial thanks go to my father, Barry, for sharing his journey with me and allowing me to lead him into this new
adventure of writing. Thank you for trusting me with
the pieces of your life's story; it's been a wonderful experience to
work together! I've learned so much.

I never would have had the courage to step out in faith and
begin this project without the support of my extended family
and my mom's encouragement to follow my heart in pursuit
of writing. Thank you for introducing me to the "She Writes"
event, what a jumping off point!

Special thanks to my sweet husband, Matt, who put up
with late nights, self-imposed deadlines, and the reading and
editing of anything I requested. I love you!

And for Izac, whose birth coincided with the birth of this
book, this will always be a special journey we took together,
even though you had no idea you were along for the ride.

My deep gratitude goes to Tate Publishing and our team
there for their encouragement and support, and to all those I've
never met, but who have touched my life through the sharing and re-telling of my father's adventure; may the Lord bless
you!

–Jodi L. Raisl

Contents

Introduction

When I was in elementary school, many kids brought stuffed animals or favorite items for show and tell; I brought my dad. I grew up listening to the stories my dad would tell of his Arctic expedition in 1970, the people he'd met, and the experiences he had. I watched presentations of slides and saw many relics from his journey. His stories stuck with me and I took great joy in sharing the tales of his wild adventure with others. I was very proud of my dad for what he'd accomplished. Through the years, however, all of the slides, journals, and artifacts slowly got filed away and became a part of family history that rarely made an appearance.

Then, in the summer of 2006, I had an idea. Would my dad be willing to share his journal and stories with me? With the intent of preserving his stories for family history, I took it upon myself to begin the process of writing this book; however, it soon became obvious the only way we could accomplish this was to work together.

Beginning in June of 2007, my dad and I began to progress on the text of the book, with him filling in the gaps that only he could, and I learning so much more about my father. I was amazed at how much he endured and how many people touched his life with hospitality and open hearts. Given the potential life-and-death situations he faced, I realized how fortunate I was to even exist!

Working with my dad on this book was an incredible experience, and I rejoice that his story, which touched me growing up, can now touch generations of readers.

May the Lord bless you as you read *It's Uphill Most of the Way Down*.

–Jodi L. Raisl

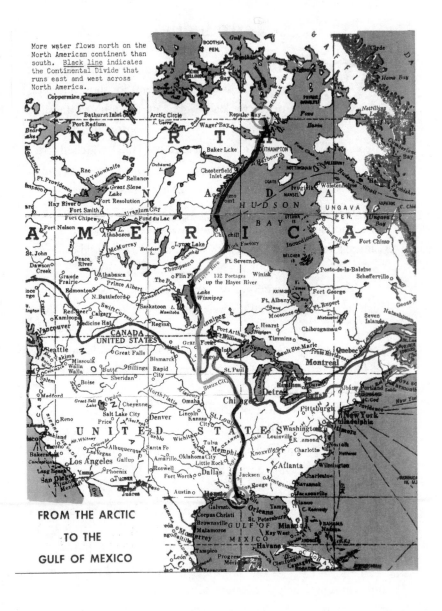

More water flows north on the
North American continent than
south. <u>Black line</u> indicates
the Continental Divide that
runs east and west across
North America.

FROM THE ARCTIC

TO THE

GULF OF MEXICO

In the Beginning

"Trust in the LORD with all your heart and lean not on your own understanding; in all your ways acknowledge him, and he will make your paths straight." (Proverbs 3:5–6)

Journal Excerpt: May 24, 1970

"Today will be the first official entry in my Schield Canoe Expedition journal. It is the first time we've been north of the Arctic Circle, our destination for starting this trek...I'm a little anxious now that I'm here and the risks I'll be facing are at hand. I pray for God's strength and protection."

From my window seat aboard the Boeing 707 now bound from Minneapolis to Winnipeg, I gazed down on the naked trees outlined with only the faintest tint of spring green and upon the miles of barren, black wheat fields of the Dakotas and northwestern Minnesota. Watching the north-flowing Red River twist and turn like a gnarled tree branch through the farmland below me, my mind drifted back over the events that had brought me here, heading to the frozen tundra of the Arctic Circle to lead the "Schield Canoe Expedition." For a young man who loved adventure and the out-of-doors, this was the opportunity of a lifetime.

It was 1969, and I had just graduated from high school and found summer work in Denver, Colorado. Given that I was only eighteen, this was my first time living away from family and all that was familiar back in my hometown in northern Minnesota. I had twelve weeks of summer before heading off to college in the fall, and I was excited to make the most of it.

Each weekend I would, by whatever means I could afford, explore one of Colorado's natural treasures. My meager budget allowed only seventeen dollars for weekend expenditures—including food and travel! So my travel options were more limited than my desire to see and experience new areas of Colorado. One weekend I made my way to Colorado Springs to see the Garden of the Gods, an area of unique and picturesque rock formations. I remembered that a former minister from my hometown church had moved there years before, and I decided to see if he was still in the area. If he was, it would probably mean a free meal and lodging for the night. Pastor and Mrs. Schield were indeed still in Colorado Springs, though it took three phone calls to locate them.

"Hello, Reverend Russell Schield?"

"Yes."

"How'd you like some unexpected company? This is Barry Lane."

Their response was an immediate invitation, and I enjoyed their warm hospitality for the weekend. It ended up being a visit that would change my life forever. During my visit, Pastor Russell tossed me an advertisement saying, "Here, you might be interested in this." On the back of a small North American map, outlined with bright blue oceans and a thick red line stretching from the Arctic Circle to the Gulf of Mexico, was the following ad:

From the Arctic Circle to the Gulf of Mexico in a canoe; through the middle of Canada and the United States, and walk less than ten miles. More miles will be traveled 'up-south' than 'down-south.' A 5,200-mile expedition for some red-blooded American boy. Anemic need not apply!

He was right; I definitely found it interesting! And so began my association with his brother, Vern Schield. He was a sixty-seven-year-old retired industrialist from Waverly, Iowa, who for two years had been dreaming of sponsoring an expedition that would retrace the routes and lifestyle of the fur traders. This journey would traverse nearly the entire continent of North America by canoe!

Many decisions confront a young person standing on the brink of independence and post high school adulthood. I was brought up in a Christian home, and I wanted to know and follow God's will for my life. I prayed for guidance and the wisdom to understand His leading—but rarely did I get a clear inkling of anything specific that God wanted me to do. Somehow this situation was different. As soon as I read the ad, my body tingled as if I'd just experienced an electric shock, and somehow, deep within my spirit, I knew that I was going to be going on this expedition. In reality, I probably wasn't qualified for the task. I'd camped and canoed all my life, but my experience was limited to the Minnesota and Canadian Boundary Waters Canoe Area (BWCA). I'd hunted for several years but only for deer and grouse. I knew little about living off the land or Arctic survival. Yet, God had placed an unmistakable certainty in my heart that I was going to be the one to canoe from the Arctic Circle to the Gulf of Mexico. I got Vern Schield's address and immediately wrote to him expressing my interest in becoming chief voyageur of the "Schield Canoe Expedition." Like a small boy anticipating Christmas Day, I endured some of the most painful waiting I've ever experienced in my life as I waited for Vern to respond.

In mounting anticipation of the trip, I began reading about the Far North, about men like Eric the Red and Henry Hudson, who had explored some of the same coastal waters I would travel. Apprehension first started entering my mind when I read things like: polar bears constantly comb the shores in search of food; Hudson Bay is inhabited by a number of species of whales including orca or killer whales; and the icy cold waters of the Arctic cause hypothermia in less than three minutes. But I was smitten and such threats were already too late to quell my interest and enthusiasm. I hadn't heard from Vern Schield yet, and although I constantly reminded myself that my chances of being selected to lead this great adventure were likely slim to none, my young heart knew better. I was captivated by the lure of this adventure—though I knew the trip would be no joy cruise. I realized that it might mean there would be times when my life would be at stake, but I had an itch inside me that said, "Go." It refused to release its grip on me. The beckoning to match wits with nature, to do the undone, and to retrace the history of the voyageurs became a goal that I did not simply want to try, but one I now felt compelled to achieve. I didn't know how or why, but somehow God had called me to this—my call to the wild.

It was six months from the time of our initial contact until I actually met the trip sponsor, Vern Schield. In January he made the trip to Gustavus Adolphus College in St. Peter, Minnesota, where I was enrolled as a freshman. I was afraid he'd come while I was attending a lecture so in the hurried moments before class I drafted one of my friends to keep an eye out for him.

"What's he look like?" my friend wanted to know.

"Looks like…I don't really know; I've never seen him," I responded.

Together we concluded that Vern would be fairly well dressed; I knew he was an elderly man, and we both gathered that he would appear to be looking for someone. With that well-rounded description established, I headed for class. Needless to say, the lecture didn't mean much. I felt utterly horrible! My head ached, my stomach was churning, and my hands were so sweaty I constantly had to wipe them on my trousers. At long last I heard my friend's faint knock, and with a pounding heart, I slipped out the nearest door.

My mind had created an abnormally large man, but there stood a very ordinary looking Mr. Schield. He wasn't a giant of a man on a white charger at all! He was of slight build in width and stature, with a commanding presence and a quiet face. My fear of fainting at our first handshake was quickly forgotten. I learned that Vern had only completed an eighth grade education. In his early years, he had eked out a living in the rock quarry he owned. He wasn't sure if it was the backbreaking work or a stroke of genius that led him to invent a movable platform for his backhoe. Whatever the reason, he had the foresight to patent his invention and had retired as a multi-millionaire. He now enjoyed traveling around the world and reading about history. It was his interest in the history of the fur trade industry and his love of travel that had spawned the idea to sponsor the Schield Canoe Expedition. We talked all afternoon, but I remember only his parting words. Before driving out of the Gustavus parking lot, he had said, "I'm favorably impressed."

I waved as he drove out of sight, then let out an undignified war whoop and exuberantly ran the perimeter of the campus in the below-zero winds. Unable to contain my excitement, I let the news of having what I called a "promising meeting" with my potential sponsor leak out to a few friends, and by morning was convinced that the campus grapevine surpassed anything Bell Telephone had yet developed. It took nearly forty-five minutes to make my way across the cafeteria to put my breakfast tray away, and I felt like a superstar when a friend of mine came and asked for my autograph. My thoughts of fame were short lived, however, when she mentioned her reason ..."Barry, can I have your autograph? I may not be here when you get back—I mean, *if* you get back!" A sobering thought to be sure.

Once Vern confirmed that he had selected me to lead the expedition, a million details and questions flooded my mind. I started wondering what would happen to my college scholarship if I were gone for a semester or more; what would I tell my parents and how would they respond; and, given the current war in Vietnam, what would the draft board do if I temporarily put my college education on hold.

I slept on the question of what to do about my current commitment to college, and the next day sat across the table from the academic dean. I had developed what I considered to be an ingenious plan. If I carried a heavy course load when I returned, and could talk the college into letting me do a number of credit-based independent studies while I traveled, perhaps I could maintain my full-time status as a student. The plan sounded good to me, but the dean was a massive man with an expressionless face that appeared to be carved from stone. I began to explain my plan to him, but the more I explained my idea, the worse it started to sound. He sat there taking it all in with long silent puffs on his pipe, and I felt like the Titanic going down by the time I finished. Suddenly, I was propelled backward by the dean's resounding slap on the table with his large fist, "By George! Maybe it's time Gustavus tried something new—a semester on the river—I like the idea. Let's not think of an independent credit or two; let's think of an independent semester—a semester on the river!" I didn't argue but left him with the mixed emotions of someone who had just had a near-death experience. This was going to be a lot of work. But the plan was set in motion; by the end of the week, I was signed up for independent studies in English, speech, geography, biology, and rather amusingly, a half-credit for canoeing and camping from the Physical Education department. I was also able to secure a letter from my local draft board recognizing that I was still *in college* and that they were aware of the fact that I was going to be out of the country for an extended period of time. With my college deferment still in effect, I knew I wouldn't be getting drafted and considered AWOL while en-route on the expedition.

My folks were always supportive of me, but I wondered what their exact reactions would be when I told them that I definitely was departing for the Arctic to return by canoe. With a tinge of envy, my dad grinned and said, "When do we leave?"

My mother, not grinning, a little pale and hesitant, asked, "Son, if I kicked, screamed, cried a lot, and asked you not to go…what would you do?"

Mustering an understanding smile as only the youngest child in a family can do, I replied, "Mom, I'd be terribly unhappy when I left."

Months passed quickly as I managed to squeeze swimming, endurance training, weight lifting, and survival reading in between college coursework. By the time March winds and April showers arrived, I was like a nervous horse waiting for the start of a race. Things started to clutter my mind. I had daily class work, exams, trip preparations, and by now, many comments conveying the same message of, "If you make it back" to brood over. I went through a period of terrible depression and self-doubt. I became convinced that I would leave on the trip but never return. It would indeed be a once in a lifetime expedition.

At ten o'clock in the evening on April 18, 1970, I hit rock bottom. I found myself sitting on a tombstone, in the darkness, in a chilly April drizzle, over a mile from campus. I was alone, confused, and no longer had the inner peace and assurance I'd had when I first learned about the expedition. Before ever dipping my paddle in the waters of Hudson Bay, I was having one of my biggest struggles—did I trust God to make this journey with me?

I'd been waking to a vivid nightmare for weeks. Its coming was so predictable I started to dread going to sleep. The sky was an endless mass of dark angry clouds that eliminated any view of the horizon and touched the turbulent water in all directions. I was deafened by the wind as it relentlessly pelted me with a mixture of rain and spray from the driven waves. My face was wet, and I could almost taste the saltiness of the water as it trickled over my tightly pursed lips. Looking at the hazy reflection of myself, I could see an engulfing fear in my eyes that one could only feel when fighting for survival. The emotions were so strong I felt sick to my stomach, as if on the verge of vomiting.

Finally, a massive wave hit the canoe with such overpowering impact it capsized. I was disoriented, submerged in the bone chilling waters of Hudson Bay. I struggled back to the overturned canoe, but already my arms and legs felt like lead weights. My cheeks tingled and were nearly void of feeling, as though numbed by Novocain. I was dying of hypothermia. I'd always wake just as my hands were sliding off the canoe for the last time. My body would be drenched in sweat and my bed sheets and blanket a tangled mess. My heart would be racing, and getting back to sleep was a process that took hours. I'd lie on my bed thinking it all seemed so real. I questioned if I knew what I was doing. I wondered what power had gained control over me that would cause me to go off on a voyage I feared and at the same time longed to experience. I no longer felt confident that this was a part of God's plan for my life. In broken despair, I lowered my rain-soaked head and prayed, because I just no longer knew. My spirit was in turmoil. In my mind I knew I might not return, but in my heart I knew I had to try, or live the rest of my life knowing I'd given up before even making an attempt.

I cannot explain how God spoke to me, but I know that evening He heard my prayers and restored my peace and confidence. Somehow He allowed me to see that this expedition wasn't going to be about my strength, endurance, or preparation—it was going to be a journey of faith. Within a moment of God-inspired insight, I knew I was going to encounter much that I could not control. I was being called to leave everything behind but my faith. After that evening, I never again doubted the success of the expedition or my safe return.

May 21 was set as the day of my departure, as well as the day of my German exam at Gustavus. It wasn't that I hadn't studied for my language test, but since that day I've often thought it must have been a benevolent professor who corrected it. I passed the test somehow, and soon I was busying myself with final preparations for the journey ahead.

As I was leaving my last morning chapel service on campus, the college president, Frank Barthe, motioned me over to the center doors, and we strolled out of the chapel with his hand on my shoulder. On the grassy lawn before us stood a host of fellow *Gusties,* and a loosely assembled pep band that struck up some rousing *go get 'em* type of football music. It was no twenty-one-gun salute, but I was flattered, turned an obvious shade of red, and felt humbled by the recognition. President Barthe gave me the blessings of the college and said, "Barry, we'd like to present you with a gift to carry with you to the Arctic." Aware of the formal nature of the college, I was expecting a pennant or perhaps a letter of some sort. To my utter surprise, President Barthe handed me a loosely wrapped piece of dried beef!

With the long piece of oily meat tucked under one arm, I stood shaking many hands in final farewells. Then I returned to the chapel with a few close friends. They held their own service for me, prayed for my journey, and presented me with a gold quarter-sized neckpiece. Engraved on it was, "With you all the way: Gott Segne Euch," roughly translated as "God bless you," and their names. I put the neckpiece on and determined not to remove it until I landed in New Orleans. My cheeks drew a little moisture as I said goodbye to my good friends.

Just three hours after my last college final, I found myself with my folks at the Minneapolis/St. Paul International Airport waiting for my departing flight to Winnipeg. "Will Barry Lane please report to the Northwest Airline desk," came over the public address system. I did, expecting some difficulty had arisen with my packs, when to my surprise some of my college friends appeared! "What are you doing here?" I asked. With twinkling eyes they led me behind a group of phone booths, where half a dozen more friends waited, guitars in hand. They sent me off with their own recently created version of musician John Denver's "Leaving on a Jet Plane."

They announced my flight, and goodbyes were said all over again. Dad gave me a firm handshake, which seemed to tell me, "I know you can do it, Son." My mom gave me a kiss and a trembling hug, which said to me, "I care about you and I'll pray nightly." We had agreed that Mom would envision me floating down a tranquil river although we both knew that wasn't likely to be a true picture of my soon-to-be daily experience. I walked slowly down the ramp to the plane but didn't look back. I wanted to, but I couldn't bring myself to do it; my focus now needed to be on the grand adventure ahead.

With the whine of the jet engines and a dart down the runway, I was off for my first stopping point, the city of Winnipeg. This wasn't my first flight, but it was about to become my most eventful travel experience to date. Within hours, I could see the city lights of the great Canadian city, slightly blurred by the gray haze of the evening. It was here that I would go through customs inspection. Crossing the United States-Canadian border had never been a difficult task, and I expected this late May evening to be no different as we walked single file past the guard and across the border. However, the Vietnam War had changed things and the border guards were now watchful for potential draft dodgers. The portly, middle-aged customs officer was asking the usual questions: "How long will you be in Canada? What's your purpose for coming?" and once in a while he would ask, "Will you have to seek employment?"

He looked into my youthful face, well buried behind a thick, red beard. "How long will you be in Canada, Son?"

"Three, possibly four months or more," I replied.

"For what purpose?" he continued.

I hesitated for a second. "Well, to be entirely truthful, I'm going to fly to the Arctic Circle and intend to canoe back as far as New Orleans."

"I see," he said twisting his lips unbelievingly. "And how old are you?"

"I'm nineteen," I replied.

"Will you take a chair over there please?" he requested, pointing to the nearest wall.

I took my place on a hard wooden bench next to a young girl trying to run away from home, and another young man suspected of draft dodging. Reviewing in my mind my comments about the coming months, I began to realize what an absurd sounding story I had just told the guard, even if it was true!

After a lengthy wait, my doubting officer returned with a

younger and leaner companion. "I understand you're going on a long trip," the younger man said.

"Yes, sir, I am," I replied.

"Can you validate this with any sort of papers?" he asked.

"Well, all the documentation I have is in my packs," I explained. Once again I answered numerous questions and restated my purpose for being in Canada for an extended period of time. By now it was obvious that they suspected me of being a draft dodger. My detention dragged on for hours. Finally, I was handed off to yet another officer, answering the same old questions and forced to tell the same unbelievable story.

"Wait a minute," the newest officer stated. "Didn't I read something about you guys in the paper? Sure, I remember now. This Schield that is sponsoring the expedition received some sort of citation from the mayor. Go ahead and get your bags…and, kid," he added as I was leaving, "good luck."

I wish I could have done what he suggested—pick up my packs. But neither of them had arrived in Winnipeg, and I was to leave for Churchill early the next morning. I described my packs to the airline clerks, used their luggage flash cards to show them samples similar to the ones I'd lost, and sent out a tracer. Wondering if fate were trying to tell me something, I hailed a taxi to take me to the Fort Gary Hotel. The hotel was an older, yet sophisticated, facility, but I had no longing for luxury; my tired body was seeking only a nice hot bath and a comfortable bed. I was staying there because that is where I was to meet up with Vern Schield. Vern had decided to travel to the Arctic to see the expedition officially get under way. At this point, all I knew was that he had been in Winnipeg for a few days finalizing arrangements for the expedition with Canadian officials. But it was already late. I would connect with Vern in the morning.

At ten the next morning we finally boarded a prop plane and headed for our next jump off point: Churchill, Manitoba,

Canada. During the flight, Vern filled me in on what had been going on in Winnipeg. Turns out the Schield Canoe Expedition of 1970 coincided with the one-hundred-year anniversary of Manitoba, Canada, and the Northwest Territories, as well as the three-hundred-year anniversary of the Hudson Bay Fur Company. As a result, Vern gained the cooperation of the Hudson Bay Company and numerous Canadian officials in transporting our supplies and publicizing the expedition. Vern also made contact with officials at Churchill and had solicited their help in securing the services of Issaluk, an experienced Eskimo guide to travel with me. Issaluk was a thirty-year-old Eskimo from Chesterfield Inlet who was to be my companion not only on the bay, but for the entire trek to the gulf.

While listening to Vern talk, I looked down at the thinly branched evergreens and the dull brown, yellow, and sickly green mosses brightened only by the occasional glare from remaining snow. An undisturbed railroad stretched its thin line across the deserted land like a string pulled taught. "*Little Eric* and the rest of the supplies went north on a train yesterday," said Vern looking over my left shoulder. "We needed to send things by rail because the last highway going north to Hudson Bay ends at the ferry crossing on Lake Winnipeg. Speaking of Lake Winnipeg, there it is."

Sure enough, there was the north end of the lake, and it was frozen solid as if surfaced with concrete. "Hope conditions are better than that next time I see Lake Winnipeg," I chuckled. "You know, Vern, that's one heck of a lot of water to canoe across."

"Shouldn't be too long until you get your first look at Hudson Bay," Vern commented, "likely that will make Lake Winnipeg seem pretty small. Hudson Bay, be it your friend or foe, will be your home for quite a long time."

When I finally got my first look at Hudson Bay, it offered

little of either comfort or distress. What I could see of the bay, as it extended out from the coast of barren, gray rock, was an uneven blanket of ice blocks and snow, both hid the true personality of the open saltwater I would soon come to know and respect.

Churchill, the end of the railway, tree line, telephone service, and the location of a nearly deserted missile site, is Canada's closest port to her wheat fields. It's a city of history, liquor, a mix of Native Canadians and Eskimos, and nearly twenty miles of paved road covered mostly by foot or the city taxi. The town had a definite personality. The people were friendly enough, but the atmosphere made me think of a scene from an early American Western. Churchill was a rough, no frills town of misfits and fortune seekers who never struck it rich, and yet they stayed here and made a place for themselves.

It wasn't long before I learned a lesson that would become an everyday experience while on the trail. In a large dirty room at the depot, I located *Little Eric,* and the other gear that arrived by rail. Inspecting the equipment, I discovered a finger-sized hole in the roof of my sailcloth tent. None of the city's three stores had anything with which to repair it. "The only repair material we have around here is a little boat fiberglass," said the helpful depot agent. Thus it was that with a square inch of cloth cut from the tent bag, and a finger coated with fiberglass, I began the practice of making do with what was available.

My being delayed as a potential draft dodger in Winnipeg, lost packs, and equipment problems forced Vern and I to delay our departure for Repulse Bay. Given the unpredictable weather in the Arctic, which could delay flights for days, and the limited number of flights scheduled to fly into Repulse Bay, being held back by even a day might push the expedition's potential start date off significantly. As if giving me a last-minute lesson on His faithfulness, my frustration with missing our intended flight to the Arctic Circle turned to thankfulness when I learned the plane we'd tried so hard to be on had crashed on its approach to Repulse Bay. Fortunately, the pilots were not seriously hurt; however, the passenger area of the cargo plane where Vern and I would have been sitting was damaged significantly.

Finally, at four o'clock in the morning of May 24, we left the Transair Airstrip of Churchill aboard a DC-3 twin-engine prop plane, a real battleship of the air streams. I swear the plane didn't take off; it vibrated off the runway! Half of the plane carried cargo; the other side carried a handful of passengers who, like us, were fastened in their worn, shaky, and loosely bolted-down seats. Most of the cargo on this flight was expedition supplies including *Little Eric*. Two of the passengers were airline representatives going north to investigate the crash landing of the DC-3 we had intended on taking to Repulse. Another gentleman, tall and thin, sporting a narrow mustache that looked as if its growth had been stunted by the cold weather, announced that he was our steward. "It's my job to serve the crummy coffee and dry sandwiches," he said, and my taste buds soon verified his judgment. Completing the list of passengers was Mrs. Dunn, an attractive young lady and the pilot's wife, who told me she was going to Hall Beach to bring back an expectant mother and two sick boys.

"You must be a nurse?" I questioned.

"No," she replied, "the only medical training I've ever had was a crash course from the doctor in Churchill yesterday. Hopefully nothing will go wrong," she added. Thus was the lifestyle of this area—do what you can to meet situations, and then accept them for what they turn out to be.

Soon we were well out over the bay. Like a piece of cracked glass, dark ribbons of water thinly coated with ice laced back and forth between the chunks, hills, gullies, and piles of ice. It wasn't until we were halfway to Coral Harbor that the ice gave way to a vast canyon of dark indigo water dotted with thousands of flat, floating islands ranging in size from that of a large rock to a several-acre island. It was a relief to see the water gently rippling like a familiar fishing lake I had often canoed in Minnesota's Boundary Waters Canoe Area (BWCA). Eventually, our flight path left the friendly blue waters, and the plane buzzed over smooth mounds of exposed rock occasionally covered by a thin blanket of snow. We descended to a small group of snowed-in buildings and an icy runway. We were in Coral Harbor, an oasis of the Arctic for those needing to refuel en-route from Churchill to Repulse.

It took twenty minutes to refuel. We stayed in the warmth and protection of the plane. Upon leaving Coral Harbor, we continued north along South Hampton Island, before heading toward the coast. We flew across the inky blackness of Wager Bay, and then returned to the blinding glare of solid ice. The glare ruined my perception and more than once I mistook the white, low hanging clouds for towering snowdrifts. Fortunately, our pilot was accustomed to the optical illusions the Arctic presents to flyers, and after circling the crash site of the DC-3 on the runway below us, he headed for the painted barrels the Eskimos had placed along a washboard piece of sea ice marking a temporary landing site. Here, roughly two miles north of the Arctic Circle, I had reached the beginning of my journey—Repulse Bay.

At Repulse Bay

"…'Love the Lord your God with all your heart and with all your soul and with all your mind.'[15] This is the first and greatest commandment. And the second is like it: 'Love your neighbor as yourself.'" (Matthew 22:37–39)

Journal Excerpt: May 25, 1970

"White men brought the Eskimo people many things that have improved their health and made Arctic life easier. We also introduced smoking, alcoholism, pollution, and welfare. In some ways it seems the primitive Eskimo culture was the more civilized."

After our perfect landing on the makeshift ice runway, we stepped out into crisp Arctic air that was much like an early winter morning in Minnesota. The plane was quickly surrounded by a crowd of Eskimo men, women, and children, a dozen snowmobiles, and a TD-20 Cat bulldozer pulling a yellow-slated trailer mounted on skis. Flights are scheduled for Repulse every two weeks, but given the unpredictability of the weather, to be within a few days or even a week of the scheduled time of arrival was considered good. While in Churchill someone had jokingly shared with me, "If you've time to spare then fly Transair." Perhaps that is why the sound of an approaching plane was celebrated by all 214 inhabitants of the village.

Looking at a people I had known only in textbooks and encyclopedias before this day was a strange experience. I felt like I was the one being given close examination. "Mister, where'd you get all those whiskers?" asked a curious dark-eyed boy. The young fellow's question caused me to realize that Eskimo men generally do not grow facial hair—and if they had any whisker hairs at all they were sparse and erratically located. Looking around at the faces peering into mine, I realized that as a white man, or kabloona, as the villagers called me, I was indeed the different one in a group of tanned faces, straight jet-black hair, and friendly yellow-toothed smiles. I was also the only one with blue eyes—an attribute they seemed to find rather fascinating. They were all bundled up in heavy pants with knee-high mukluks on their feet, giving their legs the appearance of being the same size from their waist to the ground. A quick scan of the villagers revealed few older members. I later learned that only five of the villagers were over sixty years of age, and fifty-seven were younger than the age of five! Indeed, I was the one who stood out in this place with my wild red beard, blue eyes, and youthful appearance.

I also noted few older children or teens were in the village. It seems Eskimo children are required by Canadian law to attend school like any other young person of school age; problem was, villages were so small they typically staffed only through grade five at the villages. That meant that when a child reached the age of ten or so they were flown away to Churchill, The Pas, or Yellowknife to continue their education. It was somewhat akin to sending your son or daughter off to college at the age of ten. To compound the problem, I soon discovered that many of the parents, those that had never received an education and could speak very little English, really didn't understand the process—

why the government was taking their children away. Many of them grieved the loss of their children—and for good reason. After going away and learning of doctors, lawyers, and professional careers, many of them returned to the village ill-prepared to be hunters and highly unlikely to attain a professional career. Their schooling taught them little of their own heritage, and it was my understanding that there was not a single Eskimo-speaking teacher in the Northwest Territory.

The Eskimos helped us hoist our seven hundred pounds of equipment onto the trailer. Vern had breathed a sigh of relief when Transair had agreed to fly our supplies for free rather than charging the usual cost of fifty-seven cents per pound of freight flown in from Churchill to the village. It was their way of supporting the expedition's role in celebrating the Hudson Bay Company's three hundredth year of service to the people and fur trade industry of the Northwest Territory and Manitoba's centennial. As soon as his cargo was unloaded, the pilot was anxious to get going while the weather allowed him to do so; other villages were also looking forward to the supplies and mail that were synonymous with the plane's coveted arrival. "Kid," said the pilot looking directly at me, "this is a crazy thing you're doing—good luck!"

As the large and noisy Cat crawler inched its way up the drifted banks to the town, with its engine lugging hard and spewing black smoke, we went through snow banks as high as eighteen feet deep, making me glad it was spring time in the area. The chugging of the Cat's engine and the whistle of the Arctic wind were drowned out by the whining engines of the DC-3 as the pilot lifted the metal bird back into the clear sky above us. I watched it fade to the size of a small speck in the distance, realizing at that moment everything I had worked so hard and dreamt so long about as I prepared for this arduous adventure was finally becoming reality. As my hand gripped the gunwale of *Little Eric,* I also realized this canoe was now my only way home.

My imagination ran wild as I thought of what we would encounter in the village. I thought of the igloos built by hand, the fur clothing they must wear—made from what they had hunted and killed themselves—and the dogsleds I saw myself riding behind. My stereotypical thoughts suffered a reality check when I discovered that instead of what I had pictured we were in a fairly modern little village. It was far from Beverly Hills, but it was nice, and I later learned, quite typical of modern-day Eskimo villages.

Small houses in a variety of earth tone and gray colors dotted the streets. Each home was oil heated, had electric lights, and a large picture window—although most windows were at least partially covered by drifted snow. A vacant government house in the village was designated as our temporary residence, and Vern and I were to share it with another boarder, Don McDougal. Don was a helicopter pilot who was responsible for flying supplies and mining engineers to the interior to do geological and mineral research. Several companies were mapping the tundra, so if it ever became economically feasible to mine in this area, they would be ready. I couldn't help but wonder what would happen to the Eskimos in such a scenario. Seemed they were welcome to this desolate land as long as no one else had a use for it; if it suddenly became valuable, I wondered if they would benefit from the situation or would be pushed off their homeland. The two-story structure we were taken to would have won no beauty contest for outward appearance, but its interior left me feeling very un-explorer like as I looked at its early American furnishings, green carpet, stove, and refrigerator. We had running water accessible from a large indoor holding tank, and an indoor toilet that was closer to an outhouse in form and function. The toilet resembled a sturdy metal garbage

can topped with a cheap toilet seat; it was lined with a remov-
able black garbage bag sarcastically nicknamed a "honey bag."
A large picture window overlooked the endless miles of frozen
tundra that stretched from the edge of the village (only a few
yards from the site of our building) to the horizon.

A walk around the village made me even more aware of how
dated my stereotypical expectations were. There were no cars in
Repulse, however, each family had their own snowmobile and
a komatik, or Eskimo sled. The sleds were built of one-inch
boards spaced along two-by-eight runners at least twenty feet
long. The runners were clad with a quarter-inch-thick metal
plate. The sled was held together with rope or rawhide strips
rather than nails or screws, which allowed it to move more freely
over the cement-like consistency of the uneven sea ice. All sleds
were stained with seal oil and the blood and hair of the tuktu,
or caribou. I'd soon discover riding a komatik was like sitting
on the back of a spring-less cattle truck bouncing over a rough
road, but this was a hard land, and the sled was very essential.

The flat rooftops of their homes were used as multi purpose areas: to flesh and dry hides, as garages for *kickers* (outboard motors), to store snowmobile parts, as a sun deck, and
as play area for children. A well-worn dog harness lay draped
across a snowmobile ski on one roof, an appropriate symbol of
these people, because all around me I saw an integration of the
old and new ways of life, that were tied together finer than the
threads of an intricate weaving.

The pungent odor of the air told me that the melting snow
along the shoreline had already exposed boats, sleds, and a mul-
titude of other debris from tin cans to "honey bags" containing
human waste. While not overwhelming, the definite stench of
rotting waste permeated the air. In the center of the village,
atop a hill of solid rock, was the graveyard. The plywood coffins
often poked out from their cover of large rocks, the gray splin-

tering corners evidence of the severe wind, rain, and freezing temperatures. Many of the crosses were slanted or fallen, bearing on their wind-beaten surface only an age or a few Eskimo symbols that I did not understand.

Walking past the graveyard, I encountered a team of ten dogs staked out in the snow on their individual tie lines. I love dogs and was already missing Nugget, a blonde cocker spaniel who had been my constant companion for over twelve years. For now I kept a safe distance away but could not avoid the sound of their howls. The dogs would arch their necks as though the fur on the napes of their necks had been pulled straight back; they raised, almost in unison, a long eerie cry. Listening to the answering call of other dog teams in the village, it soon sounded like a well-orchestrated symphony of mournful sounds. Perhaps they were longing for a sight of the moon, for the sky never darkened this time of year. We now had nearly twenty-four long hours of daylight; the sun would barely touch the horizon before bouncing back into the sky.

Only a few yards from our housing unit, I saw a sod hut. Upon examination I found the structure, now used for village meat storage, an example of the type of summer home villagers built before being moved to a permanent village with homes constructed of wood. Ribs from the great whales served as rafters; they were covered with caribou skins, and then topped with sod laboriously cut from the permafrost. I had no idea how old this particular structure was, but it appeared to have been there for a while and I wondered what stories it would share if given the opportunity to speak.

Eventually, overcome by weariness, I retired to my cot to rest from my travels and first-day experience in the village, but discovered I could not sleep. Eskimos apparently play all day during their months of sunshine. The happy sounds of their frolicking stirred my sleep, and I awoke to a lighted room. Yawning and bleary eyed I prepared to rise and greet the day; glancing at my watch, however, I was startled to find it was only 2:00 a.m. Breakfast, I decided, could wait for a more sensible hour!

To purchase supplies and make arrangements to travel to Chesterfield Inlet, involved working with the Hudson Bay store. The manager, Henry Voisey, was an unusual man. Having chosen to live in the Arctic for many years, he knew the area like the locals did. Henry was a legend to the town and its people. His leathery and wrinkled face told the story of his many years in the Arctic, and his quiet ways showed his patience and wisdom. Over the decades, he had served as the village emergency doctor, village administrator, business educator, English language instructor, general contractor, and peace officer. Henry offered to find two responsible Inuit (Eskimo) guides with Komatiks to travel with Vern and me as far as Chesterfield Inlet, where Issaluk was to join me. He also offered to help me gather the supplies we needed for the amount of traveling we would be doing.

Given that it would be a day or two before preparations for our departure to Chesterfield Inlet would be completed, I left the well-traveled snow of the village and took advantage of the opportunity to explore the sea ice with a young Eskimo, David Tuktujuk. Perhaps sensing my inexperience, Henry Voisey had suggested the outing as a way to better acquaint me with the Arctic. At twenty-four years of age, Tuktujuk was an advocate of the old way of life. He speared his seal with a handmade spear and traveled only by dog team. His team being well disciplined was one of the top teams of the twenty remaining in the village. It was my understanding that years ago each Eskimo had a single, individual name—no family names. Especially after 1957 when the Eskimos throughout the Northwest Territory were moved to permanent settlements, outsiders from the government and Anglican Church found them difficult to track and record. So the father's name soon became the family name, and offspring were assigned Christian names such as Mathew, David, and John for boys, and women were given names such as Sara, Rachel, and Mary. Tuktujuk preferred his Eskimo name.

Seven of the team dogs were colored with brown and white blotches, like pinto ponies. Larger than German shepherds, the dogs had thick powerful legs and seemed to have a keen intellect. I'd describe them as the Clydesdales of the dog world. Skirmishes to defend the dog's strict social position were common. As Tuktujuk harnessed the animals, he was occasionally forced to stop his work and break up a fight with the wooden handle of his forty-foot long sealskin whip.

Gem-ni-shue, the large charcoal gray lead dog, reacted instantly to Tuktujuk's command of "gee" (left), or "haw" (right). It was a bit of a disappointment to me, but Tuktujuk had never so much as mentioned the word "mush." Perhaps that was another overstated stereotype that was more romantic and imagined than functional.

Once out of the village, the dogs fanned out on the hard-crusted snow, unlike a team of horses pulling side by side, the dogs ran in a spread finger formation. I learned that this allowed each dog to run on fresh snow, avoiding that broken by the rest of the team. Also, when water filled leads appeared in the ice, capable of freezing the animal misfortunate enough to fall in, the dogs were able to find their own place and time to cross.

I watched with interest the process the dogs had to go through just to fulfill the call of nature. Even as puppies, they quickly discovered that to squat in front of a sled meant a painful nip with the whip, as the Eskimos could do without the problem of frozen fecal matter on the sled's metal clad runners. To answer the call of nature, the dogs had to jump over the traces, or lines, of the other dogs, swinging far to the left or right of the team. The team wouldn't slow down so much as a pace, which caused the dog to run and squat, run and squat, until his task was completed. Then he had to jump over the traces again, getting back to his rightful pulling position. Being a biology major, I realized the necessity of the chore, but it surely seemed like a lot of work!

We spent the entire day out on the ice, but the tired dogs pulled with renewed spirit as Tuktujuk turned them home-ward. I was as tired as the dogs from this long day's jaunt. As we stopped for the night, we enjoyed a meal of raw Arctic Char, a fish that looks like a lake trout but with the firm red meat of a salmon, to rekindle our energy.

This time of year was tenting time for most hunters, but Tuktujuk agreed to build an igloo, a talent still retained and used by hunters in the bad weather of winter. "Snow not too good," said Tuktujuk. It had to be not too hard, too soft, nor too crystalline. Finally finding some suitable snow for the chore, he cut off the top foot or more of snow, and tossed it aside. This snow was *too hard,* explained Tuktujuk. Then as if using a mold, he began cutting blocks with a carpenter saw. It seemed in no time twenty blocks appeared, all measuring six inches wide, a foot and a half high, and three feet long. The cut blocks left him standing in a coffin-sized hole in the snow. Placing a block in the middle of this, he drew a circle ten feet in diameter, from one edge of the block to the other, and as perfect as if he had used a compass. He then placed blocks along the line, shaving all four sides with a long, broad, flat knife; then they were tamped into placed until a solid ring had formed. Next, he shaved the blocks into the form of a long, curving, spiral staircase, mak-ing the first block resemble a triangle rather than a rectangle. Another layer of the same size blocks was added. All four sides were trimmed neatly with the big knife. In addition, the long surface touching the lower blocks was beveled at about thirty degrees slanting inward toward the center of the igloo.

All but a few of the blocks were carved from within the circumference of the igloo's structure. I handed Tuktujuk a block from outside the structure's perimeter, and he laughed and pointed: "Block upside down, see?" he said, turning it over. I nodded hesitantly but really couldn't understand how a block of snow that appeared to be identical on all surfaces could possibly be upside down. Tuktujuk, however, saw a subtle difference in the grain of the snow—as evident to him as the grain of wood in a finishing board would have been to me.

At last only an irregularly shaped hole about a foot across remained. It was off to the side of the seven- to eight-foot high ceiling. Tuktujuk put the final block through the hole at an angle, and holding it with one hand, beveled it until it settled into place like a cork in a bottle. We were wrapped in a solid snow cocoon with no openings until a doorway was arched out of the block previously placed across the original trench the blocks were cut from. Loose snow was packed between the joints of the blocks, and a two-inch hole was carved into the ceiling. The hole in the ceiling was for ventilation and the escape of excess heat; it would be the only opening in the igloo when evening came and the doorway was blocked. It was warm enough to remove one's parka and sit in comfort on a pile of caribou hides.

Unbelievably, the entire operation had taken only forty-five minutes, and although I watched carefully, the amazing miracle of the dome's actual construction had largely escaped me. It is still perplexing to envision or explain how one builds a round dome from rectangular blocks.

It wasn't until the morning of May 27 that the Schield expedition was to finally hit the trail. Crossing the sea ice to Chesterfield Inlet would be our first challenge. Kurok and Katoktra were to accompany Vern and me on the first leg of our trek. Kurok spoke fairly good English, but Katoktra spoke none. I wondered about the combination, for Vern and I spoke none of the Inuit language. Nevertheless, we departed. It was a far cry from my brass band departure at Gustavus, but Father Rivoirre, the village's Anglican priest, had come down to bless the canoe. His English still a bit awkward, he requested the Lord to bring our canoe "unguarded" to its destination. Able to dismiss his misspoken English, it was his warm wishes that were meaningful to us. Tuktujuk, the Voiseys, Don McDougal, and a host of the villagers came down to watch us depart. Destroying another of my childhood images, there was no rubbing of noses as Kurok kissed his wife goodbye, and then we were off.

Katoktra, straddling his snowmobile seat like a cowboy on a horse, had a rifle slung over one shoulder in the event we should see some seal or confront an approaching nanook (or polar bear). Katoktra and I led our little caravan out of the village. I rode atop a mountain of food and five ten-gallon gasoline drums wrapped in Katoktra's tent and lashed to the komatik. Kurok drove the second snowmobile, and Vern rode inside *Little Eric,* which was strapped to the second komatik. Furs and other supplies surrounded Vern, who was sitting in the canoe. While he was excited to get started, I was concerned as to if he had the stamina for the rigors of the trail that lay ahead.

When I first saw the food supplies we'd packed, made up largely of tea, corned beef, and hard tack, I thought it was far too much, but with his vintage wisdom, Henry explained it this way: "This trip should take four days. That means you plan for eight and hope it doesn't take more than twelve. That's how it is in the Arctic."

With men like Henry around, I was quick to learn Arctic patience and its importance. In the Arctic you don't eat, sleep, and travel on a timetable. You eat when you are hungry, travel in good weather, and sleep when you are tired or trapped in bad weather. Above all, I recognized the importance of relying on the sound judgment of my experienced companions. The first thing they explained to me on the trail was why we traveled so late into the evening. During the day, the snow was sticky and caused the snowmobiles to overheat. Even the slightest change in the position of the sun was enough to alter the temperature, even if the amount of daylight remained fairly consistent. So we waited for later hours, firmer snow, and cooler temperatures. When day was upon us, we migrated to the rock shore, where the sun warmed our tent and the wind-polished granite we slept on. I could see that the wealth of knowledge I could gain from these men would be invaluable. Later events were to bring that fact home pointedly.

Anything I'd read about the Eskimo people of the Northwest Territory that was printed prior to 1957 was outdated. I now questioned the historical accuracy of much of what I'd studied. For example, the books I'd read created the impression that seal and walrus were staples of the Eskimo diet. The truth is that seal and walrus smell and taste a great deal like cod liver oil. I doubt that it ever has tasted very good. In a land where Arctic Char, caribou, and ptarmagen abound, seal and walrus were not eaten. In villages where dog teams were still active, the meat was given to the dogs; however, given the decline of dog teams, the carcass was now typically left for other wildlife to devour once the valuable skin or walrus tusks had been removed. At least among the Eskimos I traveled with, they would need to be starving before they would have considered eating either seal or walrus meat.

I hadn't been here long, but I sensed something about this land. Something wild and beautiful that even the most structured settlement couldn't tame. The Eskimo people were wonderful. Without realizing it, they were environmentally conscious. Nearly everything from a caribou kill, including the meat, bone, bone marrow, sinew, and hide, was used. They were resourceful; they survived in a barren land that had no trees and for most of the year was nothing but ice and snow. And they were innovative—constantly amazing me at how, without formal education, they had become skilled at using modern technology such as snowmobiles and firearms to enhance their lives. What troubled me was how "civilization" had interrupted and tarnished the good things I associated with their way of life. In many respects, it appeared Canada was making the same mistakes with the Eskimos that Americans had made with Native Americans—robbing them of both their heritage and dignity. In my heart, I vowed I would not make that mistake. While I was living with them, I would seek to understand and respect their ways.

The cargo plane delivers Barry and his supplies to the Arctic.

The igloo Tuktujuk and Barry made. It took them forty minutes.

On the Trail

"…let the wise listen and add to their learning, and let the discerning get guidance …" (Proverbs 1:5)

Journal Excerpt: May 31, 1970

"The Lord has been rich in allowing me to experience the Arctic, and merciful to me in my inexperience."

We made good time across the sugar-like crystals of snow, for they were packed as hard as concrete by the wind. The ice fields and pressure ridges made travel more difficult. We passed through areas that looked like hundreds of crumbling snow forts, and rode over mounds of ice that the tides and winds had pushed up like the center of a freshly baked pie. Huge irregularly shaped blocks of sea ice in shades of blue to sea green were piled along the coast in sizes varying from that of an automobile to that of a large house. Several feet of pure white snow often topped these mammoth pieces of colored glasslike structures resembling an overabundance of whipping cream.

Every four hours we would stop for two or three cups of tea. Drinking warm tea prevents a chill, and helps a person to stay warm for about three to four hours. An Eskimo won't even drink tea when it is hot, for that makes you sweat, and you eventually get colder. If the tea is too hot, he'll add a little snow to cool it. If hunger gripped us during a tea stop, a can of corned beef was dug out from within our tightly wrapped supplies. We usually settled for tea and Pilot Biscuits, a hard tack that I'm sure was part brick and tasted to me like it was partially made of cardboard!

At one stop, running his finger around a peninsula shown on our maps to extend far out into the inlet, Kurok said, "Too far—maybe not enough gas to make it. This way we go," he said tracing a series of low spots across the peninsula. We headed inland.

It wasn't that I was so tired, although I was becoming bow-legged from straddling ten-gallon drums of gasoline strapped to the komatik, but a body can remain in one position only so long. Having reached my limit, I stretched my form out on top of our supplies. I intended to remain there only until my legs regained some feeling, but I fell asleep as we continued to roll along at freight train speed. I awoke suddenly from a painful blow, as my head slammed viciously into the tundra. My right cheek was lying tightly against a blood-spattered rock. Fortunately, my pride was hurt more than anything as I rose to brush myself off. My fall put an inch-long cut under my right eye and took a generous portion of skin from my nose and cheek. It was amazing I hadn't broken my jaw. When I put my glasses back on, I found that one lens had several scratches on it.

"Are you all right?" asked Vern, as he, Kurok, and Katoktra came running up.

"I'm fine," I replied, "but I just learned another Arctic law—don't ever fall asleep on a komatik!"

About fifteen miles into the peninsula, our trail seemed blocked. Following the only snow route we could find brought us to the brink of a high, steep, snow-filled ravine surrounded by sheer cliffs. We had no alternative trail to follow, and we did not have sufficient gasoline to retrace our steps to the coast, not if we were going to make it to Chesterfield Inlet.

Kurok slid down the steep incline and checked out a ninety-degree corner banked with snow like the curve of a bobsledding track. "River down there," said Kurok, pointing beyond the deadly bend. "We get to river, be okay." First the snowmobiles were carefully maneuvered down the bank to the river, where Vern was left anxiously standing as if to wave the checkered flag at the end of a great race. With adrenalin pumping, Katoktra, Kurok, and I grunted and strained to get the heaviest komatik up the incline to the brink of the cliff. As if it were a teeter-totter, we held the sled in perfect balance for a moment before we shifted its weight slowly forward and began the downward plunge. Digging in the heels of our feet to reduce the speed of our descent seemed as futile as pulling back on a runaway railroad car. My heart pounded wildly in my throat, I prayed, "God, slow us down!" It appeared the weight of the gasoline drums on the sled and the tremendous speed we had gained was going to end with an explosive slam into a solid wall of granite. The gap closed quickly until only a sled length of snow remained. The runner of the komatik kissed the wall of the ravine before it twisted sharply downhill, falling to the safety of the river ice. Little was said aloud, and after a short rest, we climbed back up the face of the cliff for the other sled, knowing that the results could be different this time. With exhausted bodies, we labored to get the komatik bearing *Little Eric* to the brink of the cliff, and began our uncontrolled race downhill. This time the sled was lighter and had a semi-broken trail to follow. On this attempt we were sure we would miss the corner wall. The first time God had been merciful.

We followed the safety and comfort of the Snow River to the bay, where we were forced to maneuver around masses of icy rubble stacked in haphazard formations along the shoreline. We began encountering open leads in the ice, often one to three feet wide and filled with water. After catapulting one of the larger leads or cracks in the ice, Vern commented, "Thank heavens I was in the canoe." Even though he had grinned, I could tell our rigorous travels, limited diet, and primitive camping conditions had challenged his endurance more than Vern had expected. He looked tired and stressed.

Pointing to the horizon, Kurok drew my attention to the sky. Half the sky was light blue; toward the southern horizon, the haze was heavier, and the sky stained a heavy navy blue. "Wager Bay open," said Kurok with a rather distressed tone and a strained look on his weathered brown face. "We go inland again—not good," he continued. Perhaps we were the first to get a glimpse of what we now call global warming for we were ground to a dry and snow-less halt less than 2,000 feet inland from the coast. We gathered around one of the sleds, unfolding a well-creased topographical map. After much discussion in the mixed tongues of Eskimo—part Eskimo and English—we headed back toward the ever-increasing danger of the melting coastal ice. We were going to get as close to the open water of Wager Bay as we dared go. I realized that we would be forced to wait there until open water reached us and we could continue by canoe. We were not going to make it to Chesterfield Inlet.

As we made camp, it was evident we were all weary. Vern had taken the hours of rough travel as well as could be expected at his age; however, he was the first to admit that the prospect of retracing all those miles back to Repulse Bay was more than he thought he could handle. After much debate, it was decided that he and I would remain at Wager Bay while Kurok and Katoktra returned to Repulse. At first it might have seemed wiser to have Kurok or Katoktra stay at Wager Bay with us, but this was the situation. In this land, traveling alone is comparable to swimming alone—possible, but not a good idea.

Vern was the last choice to return to the village by snowmobile because of the wear he had suffered going only one way. There was the possibility of soon being able to reach Wager Bay from the south by canoe; in this case it seemed most sensible that I remain at Wager Bay with our supplies, waiting for Issaluk and a companion to join me from the south. Therefore, we decided Vern and I would remain at our present position while Kurok and Katoktra returned to the village with the following message: *"Open water—present position approximately eighty-seven degrees five minutes east by sixty-five degrees twenty-five minutes north. Request supplies and air evacuation of Mr. Schield—currently all is fine."*

The next morning, feeling some hesitation and responsibility for leaving two Kabloonas, or white men, alone in this harsh land, especially with a limited food supply, Kurok went hunting. I had observed him seal hunting before, and it is almost an art form. The Eskimo wears a double parka, the thinner outer parka being of a canvas material, which breaks the cruel windy weather, and a thick inner parka of army blanket type material, which I found had more uses than just that of warmth. Seeing a seal, the hunter removes his dark colored outer parka, and in his white inner parka, fades into the snow like a polar bear. He begins a straight-line approach to the netserk, or silver seal. With his .22 rifle held in front of him and riding belly down on a two-foot komatik resembling a child's toy sled, or simply crawling, he slowly makes his approach from as much as a quarter mile away. Never moving left or right, he travels with slow, steady progress. But the seal is a restless sleeper, raising its head frequently for a cautious look around. If distracted by the hunter, the uneasy animal will arch his head high, peering intently at the Eskimo. Hardly drawing a breath, the Eskimo will lie still for a half minute. But his alert prey is not always so easily fooled. The hunter sometimes has to arch his own head and even move his feet like flippers. If his act is good, the net-serk resumes its rest and the hunter his slow trek toward it. Sometimes the hunter gets within fifty or sixty feet before the fatal slug is slammed into the animal. It has to be the perfect kill—a headshot because wounded animals lurch their fatty bulk into the hole instinctively to escape danger.

Kurok returned within an hour with a seal. The seal, which is almost inedible unless one is starving, and some previously killed Ptarmigan would have to be the mainstay of our diet should Kurok and Katoktra be delayed by accident or bad weather. Parting with a rifle was like losing a friend to these hunters, and even our unfortunate circumstances made it diffi-cult to decide which hunter would leave us the protection of his firearm. We all realized both parties needed a rifle in the event of a bear, and should a problem arise…it would be vital for securing food. We divided our supplies. A quick inventory told me Vern and I had perhaps enough food and fuel for a week. It should take only three days for the men to return to the village barring any difficulties. Vern and I watched, listened, and prayed as our only human contact for two hundred miles moved out of sight. I decided that while our position was uncomfortable, I couldn't change it, so we'd make the best of it—no complaints, no dramatic fits of fear, just a simple striving to survive. I was indeed conforming to the attitude this land instills in those who live here.

On the second day after our companions left, and want-ing a better view of Wager Bay, I departed camp for a look around the area. The tundra looked the same for miles, and the bare rock left no trace of boot prints. I saw nothing grow-ing over three inches high, but more than half of this inland area was covered with delicate, brightly colored plants. Lichens grew in close-knit blotches of green, black, and orange on most of the rocks, and grass and moss filled the low points between the rocky hills. Flowers resembling miniature roses, daisies, and plants that looked like shrunken tumbleweed were all growing with springtime vigor only inches from remaining patches of snow. I slowed my pace to observe five Ptarmigan strutting only twenty feet away, tossing their heads and causing their red combs to flop, spreading their black and white tail feathers as if a fan. About two miles from camp, I spotted four caribou, prancing like Santa's reindeer near a light blue lake of melted snow. They were in the process of changing from their winter white coats to a darker summer color. Against their off-white faces, the black outlining of their lips was especially visible. Their horns had a mossy brown covering and each had stockings of brown and black. They trotted away as I approached, turning often to watch me with curiosity. I hadn't intended to make this a hunting trip, but when four big rabbits caught my eye I decided it wouldn't hurt to add one to our food stores. Still wearing all white, they were easy to spot against this snowless area of tundra. I took aim down the rusted sights on the barrel. My shot was off the mark and the rabbits disappeared. I could live with that, but the gun had jammed—a problem that could have serious consequences. I immediately dropped to the ground and spent the next hour trying to free the shell casing. I was unsuccessful, and from now until someone returned by snowmobile or helicopter, we would have no firearm to protect against the potential of a polar bear attack.

As I approached our camp, I heard the happy mechanical "whish-whish" of a helicopter. It flew over us and landed only a few hills away, near the yellow signal blanket I had put out to mark our camp and an appropriate landing site. The chopper pilot was Don McDougall, our bunkmate at Repulse Bay. With the undependability of radio and instruments for flying the bush-less *bush* country this far north, pilots rarely venture out unless the ground is visible, allowing them to navigate by topographical map and landmarks. Bad weather had settled in to the north of us, and Don hadn't been able to leave Repulse Bay for a camp he served in the interior. It was a pure stroke of luck that he was still in the village when Kurok and Katoktra had arrived. With nothing but an unblemished sky stretching overhead, he had been free to fly south to our position with Kurok riding along as his guide. This truly called for a celebration—tea, hard tack, and all the corned beef we could eat, which if you were sensible wasn't very much.

Don lifted a note out of his flying jacket and handed it to Vern. With a blank look of having hit another roadblock, Vern read it and then handed it to me. The letter was from Tagak Curley, Eskimo Administrator of Repulse Bay, and Henry Voisey, the elderly Hudson Bay Company manager in the village. It read: *Having discussed the situation with various responsible and knowledgeable persons in the settlement, we have decided that it would not be advisable for Mr. Lane to remain at Wager Bay by himself. Therefore, we have sent Kurok to assist Mr. Lane in caching supplies at Wager Bay. Arrangements have been made for two snowmobiles and men to come for Mr. Lane and Kurok as soon as possible. Due to the potential hazard of one man staying alone, we request you follow our advice.* Vern and Don were soon gone, trying to take advantage of fair skies and favorable winds. Kurok and I would need to wait at least two days for the snowmobiles to arrive.

As tired as he was from his hard travels, Katoktra had volunteered to return to our camp with Amilek, another Eskimo guide. As soon as they arrived, we crowded into the warmth and shelter of our tent and boiled up some tea on our rusty Coleman. I'd swear that the hard tack was getting even worse. They were so dry that too large a bite would give me a headache as I struggled frantically to swallow it. The tent was full of chatter; however, I was the only one in the tent not speaking Eskimo and, logically so, the only one not too sure of what was going on. I gathered it had been agreed that Katoktra and Amilek would rest for a while, and then we would have to leave, for it was nearly a week since our departure from Repulse and the ice in this area was bad and getting worse—a few more days and it could possibly move out leaving us stranded.

While Katoktra and Amilek rested, Kurok and I started to cache or store supplies. At the top of the hill behind us was a twenty-foot crevasse about a foot wide. We laid our supplies in it, and then carried *Little Eric* to the hilltop. We turned it upside down over our packs, snuggly pushing the high bow and stern into the crack. Next, we roped it down securely to a dozen rocks as large as we could possibly carry. With this task done, we woke our colleagues and headed north. I'd have to return to Repulse Bay, and fly south to Chesterfield Inlet where Joe Issaluk and I would travel north to Wager Bay by canoe to recover *Little Eric* and the supplies we'd just left in cache. To be headed north again was a disappointing feeling. My goal was to head south at nearly any cost.

I was shocked at the changes that had already taken place in the sea ice. What had been as solid as concrete was now covered with water and an inch of slush. Replacing the loud "whack" of the iron runners on hard ice was a splash like that of a slow boat bouncing on small waves. Snow drifts once comparable to large white-capped waves could no longer even pass for ripples. What had been a blinding reflection of snow was gone, replaced by the dull gray or light blue of weakened ice. Many open leads crisscrossed in front of us, outlined in light blue, but filled with deathly cold indigo water. The lead where we had our trouble on the way down, now stretched before us as an impassable river of open water nearly twelve feet wide. We searched two miles before we found our only hope of reaching the other side. With two feet of open water on our side and the far bank barred by nearly three feet of open water, a large room-sized ice pan floated in the still dark river. For us it was an island of hope.

Taking up the nearly thirty feet of slack in the towrope between the machine and the sleds, each snowmobile took a daring jump. Kurok and Amilek were the first to make it safely across. Katoktra and I sat waiting for the island to stop its ship-like rocking. With his machine darting past me, Katoktra was safely to the middle, but his machine came to a sudden teetering stop on the far edge. The skis had cleared the lip of the opposite ice bank, but his rubber track had just barely gripped it, the bulk of the machine churning the water like an outboard motor. Throwing his body far out over the handle bars, yet remaining on his machine, Katoktra slowly crawled forward over the edge, giving my Komatik a sudden jerk which shot it forward, spanning first one crack and then the other. Our worst crossing was over.

The wind was cold, and Kurok, in his hasty return by helicopter, didn't bring back sufficient clothing. I loaned him my full-body nylon shell and some long underwear, then donned my extra pair of pants and slipped into my poncho, which I felt would help cut the wind. None of the Eskimos had ever seen a poncho, and I thought they were going to die of laughter. "Look like the father," said Kurok, referring to Father Rivoirre, the Anglican priest at Repulse.

We pushed hard to take advantage of the weather, covering two hundred miles of difficult terrain in eleven hours. We stopped to warm ourselves with tea, and I listened to their broken English as they told how their ancestors had stalked polar bear with only a knife, circling the animal like a pack of dogs, trying to stay behind him, where they would slash at the area behind the foreleg in hopes of striking the heart. I was surprised to hear that bear liver is never eaten or even fed to the dogs. Later I found it had the potential to kill because of its high vitamin A content. I listened with anxiety to their talk of Wager Bay, understanding from their talk that currents were terribly strong. "Times bear no can swim," said Amilek. "Too strong."

Sitting on the sled for at least four hours at a time, my feet became so cold, I'd look down to see if I was wearing only street shoes. Each time I would find I still wore wool socks, felt liners, and Canadian packs. I noticed Katoktra and Amilek wore boots exactly like mine, but neither of them had any laces. I attributed this to the fact that they either couldn't afford them or the bay store had no laces. I finally understood, however, and loosened my boots three-fourths of the way down. I was amazed as my feet became warmer within the half hour; bottled up in a waterproof, tightly laced boots, the moisture can't escape, causing one's feet to be cold.

About fifty miles from Repulse, we stopped at an island to visit a hunting party I understood to be Katoktra's relatives. Near the edge of the island lay a team of off-white huskies whose fur was accented with tangled clumps of matted hair. The dogs seemed rather unconcerned about our approach. An old weather-beaten snowmobile sat between two soiled white tents to our right, and an equally sooty tan tent to our left. Stepping through the three-foot high door of one of the tents, I felt like I had gone back in time. The structure was about fourteen by twelve and perhaps six feet high, being supported at each end by a notched pole. A thin wooden center beam ran the length of the canvas roof and fit into the notch of the end poles. With each gust of wind, the poles creaked, straining to pull out of the pile of rocks, which held their base in place. The once white canvas was hidden beneath layers of soil and soot, and at least three holes, which looked like cigarette burns, allowed narrow lines of light to stream in from the outside. The tent was floorless, the edge being held down by a foot-wide rock flap, weighted every two feet with a head-sized rock.

In the middle of the barren and uneven granite floor, sat a single burner Primus stove with a small yellow flame. Along the back of the tent, the entire family slept on three layers of caribou hide turned upward toward their naked or lightly clad bodies. With the exception of a teenage boy, the entire family—father, mother, one young boy of about seven, and his sister of nearly the same age, and a young baby girl—all lay covered with two quilts. The father and eldest son rose and greeted us. The father wore a once white T-shirt, now gray, and as he rose to dress, I saw he wore nothing else. The mother wore an equally soiled light yellow nightgown, and the three children were naked.

Strewn on the floor were unwashed kettles, cups, a blood-stained knife, and a half moon-shaped ulu used by Eskimo women to do everything from cut bread to skin seals. Empty corned beef cans, Pilot Biscuit boxes, bare white bones, and three half-eaten lemmings were scattered around the tent along with a handful of burned matches, cigarette butts, and ashes. In one corner was the half-eaten carcass of a caribou; the smell of its raw meat made my stomach churn. Piled against the back wall of the tent was an un-fleshed caribou hide. Much to my surprise, two house cats strolled into the tent. In typical cat behavior, they strolled right over to a piece of meat, bending occasionally to sniff indifferently at its drying surface. I have no doubt that the meat was still eaten for supper. The woman wiped out some soiled cups with a dirty rag and poured us some scalding coffee, strong enough to melt a spoon—had I had one! Since it was both strong and hot, I felt some hope that it would kill the germs in my grimy cup.

The men and women from the neighboring tents soon joined us, and I felt awkward in the midst of eleven rapidly talking Eskimo people. I knew Kurok was telling them about my poncho, and I laughed along with them. I handed Katoktra my strong prescription sunglasses as he sat looking at his own broken sunglasses. He started to weave as if drunk, jabbering a mile a minute after he tried them on. All laughed, and the glasses were passed around the circle as if they were some sort of peace offering that was to be shared by all.

Much to the mother's disgust, her little one wet on the Caribou mats. Using her soiled nightgown, the mother roughly yet affectionately, wiped the child's bottom, and then reaching for the bleached shoulder blade of a caribou she spooned the urine into an empty can. Apparently not the youngster's day, she then knocked her bottle onto the rock floor, and out of her own reach. As I handed it to the mother, I could see through the black fingerprints that covered the bottle what appeared to be a mixture of instant milk. Wiping the nipple with her unwashed hands, the mother smiled and returned the bottle to the child.

Once we were back on the trail, I assumed we would push on to reach Repulse Bay. Much to my surprise, about twenty miles from the village my colleagues decided to stop and make camp. Even with our obvious language barriers, I was able to convey my sentiments about stopping, "The village is close, let's keep going."

Kurok conveyed, "Hungry and tired now."

"But, the village is only twenty miles away," I stated. "Don't you want to get back to the village?"

All three laughed and jabbered among themselves. Finally, Kurok communicated a question to me that conveyed what they found so funny. "Kabloona think village won't be there tomorrow?"

They were right. We were all tired and hungry, and yes, the village would still be there tomorrow. I'd already learned much from these wise people that had for so long survived the desolation and harsh realities of the Arctic, but stepping back from the hard-pushing American lifestyle was a mindset I hadn't yet fully embraced

The expedition travels by komatik.

A lunch of raw Arctic Char on the trail.

Back to the Village

"For I know the plans I have for you," declares the LORD, "plans to prosper you and not to harm you, plans to give you hope and a future."
(Jeremiah 29:11)

Journal Excerpt: June 2, 1970

"My early impressions of the Eskimo people—They travel in good weather, sleep in bad, kill when game is present, and eat when hungry. They can turn stone into beautiful carvings and hides into useful garbs. They are adaptive, excellent hunters and navigators, survival experts, and very family-oriented and trustworthy."

Destined to make Repulse Bay my home for a time, I set out to learn all I could from the people that lived here. I found that Tagak Curley, the administrator, was a good source of information. So I was especially glad when he invited me to his house for a dinner much different than the corned beef and Pilot Biscuits I had become accustomed to on the trail.

Tagak's wife, Anna Louise, was a pretty young Anglo-Saxon from Holland who had a warm smile and big blue eyes. She was wearing a splashy, purple mini-skirt, which seemed out of place in a community located miles north of the Arctic Circle.

Standing next to her was another attractive woman not much older than me. Inga Henderson, a German, was the school-teacher's wife. Both women had come to northern Canada for the experience, planning on staying just a year. As things turned out, Anna met Tagak at the Churchill hospital where she worked and now found the Arctic Circle was her home address. Inga's story was similar. She had met Rob Henderson, a bright young man committed to working as a teacher among the Eskimos, and she too now made her permanent home in the far north.

I appreciated both the company and the meal. While I was doing well at deciphering the meaning of Eskimo words, it was relaxing to be in a group where everyone spoke relatively good English. I missed my college friends and the endless conversations we had about everything from world events to romantic interests and future career aspirations.

As soon as I entered Tagak and Anna's home, the wonderful aroma of homemade bread overwhelmed me. I had to use restraint, or I'd have eaten the entire plate of fresh bread placed on the table. I hadn't smelled anything that tantalizing since leaving home. The bread was complemented by a saucy and well-seasoned bowl of pink Arctic Char. I couldn't help but smile; sitting at a linen covered table and eating the char with a fork was a far cry from how we'd eaten it on the trail. Kurok and Katoktra had held the pieces of raw fish in their teeth, slicing the salmon-like meat rapidly with their perfectly edged hunting knives, cramming the meat into their mouths with the blade of the knife. In an attempt to save my nose and throat, I had attacked the meat a bit more gingerly. I wasn't confident about eating from a sharp hunting knife, and I had suspicions about the minute parasites I could be consuming along with the raw fish. Without a doubt, the tender pieces of cooked fish and fresh bread Anna and Inga had prepared were much more to my liking than those hard stale Pilot Biscuits and raw char.

I wanted to learn more about the people, their history, and what the future may hold for them, and I thought Tagak would be good to talk with, as he was one of the more educated Eskimos of the Northwest Territory.

"Times have changed since I moved into the village," he said. "A boy was once expected to be a man at around the age of ten, capable of hunting, trapping, and surviving in the barrens. But now these skills are not so highly developed, for boys are sent down south to school. Many of the older people in this village have never seen a real tree, or like me, they were at least twenty years old before they did. Now the young ones see such things when they leave the village."

"It is rather sad," said Rob, who had joined our discussion, "that there isn't an Eskimo-speaking teacher in the Northwest Territory. The kids are taught to read, write, speak, and think English. Really, when the children return, they are no more Eskimo than you or me."

"It's a shame the children aren't taught more of their own culture and background," said Tagak. "On the other hand, I want an education for my people so a boy who wants to be a doctor or a dentist can become one."

Rob chimed in, "Which makes it a rather vicious circle right now, for rarely do they receive enough training to go on to anything other than perhaps a technical school. They are no longer fit for the tundra and yet they aren't prepared to go into any high-paying professional occupation. And the older ones still haven't had things explained to them clearly. It will be at least a generation before such a wide gap is narrowed, when those in school now are the adults."

"Boy," I said, thoughtfully reflecting on what had been said, "it's sort of sad to see such a fascinating way of life disappearing."

"It is changing, but it may not disappear," Tagak replied.

"This country demands a certain lifestyle, as you are rapidly learning. We have our own culture, and I think we will preserve it. Already many men are returning to dog teams because of the expense and repairs on snowmobiles."

I asked Tagak about the demographics of the village. He identified two primary reasons for the short life expectancy among the villagers; unlike America, tuberculosis was still prevalent in this area, and Eskimos had very limited access to medical and dental care. "Guess that explains the yellow teeth," I stated.

"Yes," said Tagak, "if they have any teeth at all."

Rob had quite an interest in the Eskimo people and was also a valuable source of information. "I've always found their naming system rather fascinating," Rob told me. "The people really have only one name. And like everything else in this country, things are changing, but in the past, and still to some extent, the children are named after recently deceased ancestors. For example, here in the village, a five-and-a-half-year-old girl was named Attowa after her grandfather. Because she bears his name, it is believed she continues his spirit; therefore, she is treated with the utmost of respect as her grandfather would have been, and because her grandfather enjoyed smoking, she has been taught to smoke heavily. With some people holding onto taboos and such old rituals, while others entirely abandon them, it's hard to talk of cousins or aunts or uncles because it really doesn't fit into their culture."

Rob continued, "Respect and taboo have always been well engrained in this culture. One taboo, which is now nearly dead, is a man's reference to his wife's mother. He may call her *my wife's mother,* or *my mother-in-law,* but he is not to refer to her by her proper name. I've never really understood why."

Marriage was another point of interest in our conversation. "Most marriages now," Rob continued, "are done within the realm of the church, but when living as nomads, where they met other families only a few times each year, pre-arranged marriages with a trial period were common. The man usually moved in with his wife's family for perhaps two months. If things appeared to work out, then they became man and wife—if not, he moved out. In the event a child was born, the baby merely became a part of the girl's family. Even now, men from the small villages go to other villages to find a wife. For example, one young man from Repulse had just gone to Igloolik in search of a bride."

While Tagak and Rob were valuable sources of information about Eskimo culture, nothing replaced firsthand observation and experience. The village was always bustling with activity. I watched as the women scraped remnants of meat and fat from the tuktu or netserk skins, firmly holding the bone or wooden handle of their half moon-shaped ulu in calloused hands. The women vigorously worked the seal hide back and forth between their hands or chewed on it, making it pliable enough to make boots. The sewing was all done by hand, using the same sinew stripped from the back of the caribou. Resembling monofilament fishing line, it would not rot or break in the wet weather. I watched them make parkas and boot liners. When not working the skins, one could see them chiseling away at the waxy gray surface of soap stone, turning out magnificent carvings of hunters, seals, musk ox, or other things that were a part of their lives. These scrimshaw figurines would be sold to Father Rivoirre who ran a cooperative for the people, seeing that their crafts got to the markets in the south.

I observed that business concerning running the village was generally a problem handled by the women, for the men spent most of their time out in the tundra foraging game and food for their families. But the men kept busy when they were in town. They worked miracles piecing together snowmobiles of all makes, even though they lacked formal mechanical training. Those with dog teams, such as Tuktujuk, spent time mending and untangling harnesses and lines. When time allowed, many men worked skillfully at the soapstone or carefully formed metal spearheads. "The men think of bird when forming the shape of the spearhead," Tagak told me, holding up one he himself was making. "The barbs are like the bird's tail, and the angle between the barbs and point should be that of a bird's back."

The daily focus of the villagers was on food, shelter, clothing, and the hunt. Putting money in the bank, building better homes, or trying to get ahead of the "Joneses" wasn't a part of their simple, survival culture. In Repulse they had no locks on their doors, for their neighbors would not steal. To take what another man needed or to desecrate the cache he'd left on the trail was unthinkable. The strict code was not to steal it! Rob Henderson, the teacher I'd met, said the kids were so honest that if they cheated in school, they would tell you.

Running into Father Rivoirre one day, I asked him about the Eskimo outlook on death. "They live a simple faith, living life as it comes, and accepting death as something the fate's hand to all," he explained. As we continued walking together, I inquired about a black balloon-like object anchored to a rock near one of the Eskimo homes. It resembled a swollen seal with a short stick plugging its mouth.

"What is it?" I asked. "It looks like a seal."

"It is," Father stated. Then he explained how they cleaned out the entire animal, to the outer hide, through the mouth. Once the animal's flesh and bone structure has been removed, the anus was sewn shut. After that, it was blown full of air and the mouth hole plugged. Even the hairy flippers are left on making it appear to be a very bloated seal or a large misshapen beach ball. "The people use that as a float for tracking harpooned walrus and whale; some men now use barrels instead," explained Father.

Hours of steady cold drizzle had caused the snow to quickly turn to icy mush. As the massive drifts of snow surrounding the village melted, it either pooled among the rock or ran like a river to the sea. I watched a young boy, using oversized garbage bags as boots, wade into the river-like streets, and race a little stick boat down the swiftly moving stream. The wind, which had been so biting and penetrating during our travel on the ice, was now so mild I was comfortable wearing only my wool jacket, without a parka. As the snow left, tons of garbage, ranging from tin cans and snowmobile parts, to raw meat and broken honey bags lay exposed everywhere. Tagak had told me about this growing problem. When living as nomads on the tundra (or even when traveling) the floorless tents were moved frequently, and the garbage was left behind. Then, when the people were brought into a permanent settlement by the government, they were not taught how to dispose of their refuse. So, as was their custom, they just threw it outside. But now they weren't moving every few weeks or months, so the garbage kept piling up. Tagak was teaching the people—his people—how to solve their own problems. "It comes slowly sometimes," he said, "But they are recognizing their own problems and asking what to do about them. Shortly the garbage will be cleaned up I think."

"I hope your canoe is well tied down," said Tagak. "I got a weather report through today from Chesterfield Inlet and they say eighty mile per hour winds have hit the Wager Bay area." With that I swallowed hard. At the time we secured *Little Eric* I thought we did a good job, but now I wondered. Such winds could easily carry the canoe away. I imagined returning to the splinters of *Little Eric* beaten and scattered all over the tundra.

Henry Voisey, who had joined our conversation, added, "If this weather keeps up, the ice will be breaking up in July. The earliest thaw I remember was some years ago on the sixteenth of July. Usually the inlet isn't clear until August." Given that Henry had been in the Arctic for decades, his observation was significant.

Since our return from Wager Bay, contact with even the nearest island had been scant. Repulse had been isolated—inaccessible by air or water, and without any outside communication. Communication over the radio, much like our ability to travel, depended entirely on the weather.

Things can change quickly in the Arctic. When the weather breaks, everything comes alive. Much to our surprise, our friend Don, the helicopter pilot, flew into Repulse from the geologist camp 160 miles away. He too had been pinned down by bad weather and was just now able to get out. We were even more surprised that evening at 11:30 p.m. when an eight-passenger Islander maneuvered out of the sky into Repulse. After many weeks of no visitors, we had two welcomed visits in one day! Unfortunately for Vern and me, this was not our ticket out. The pilot had bucked strong winds, landing only long enough to refuel and pick up the teachers and two very sick Eskimos. "Any chance of me tagging along?" Vern asked the pilot. "I'd even be willing to pay a little extra."

Looking at his load and the heavy winds, the pilot answered firmly, "Nope, there's no way anyone tags along on this flight."

The following day brought yet another bright surprise. As I was helping Don unpack some of his supplies from the helicopter, a small Aztec airplane appeared in the sky. The plane brought a doctor and a nurse, who visited Repulse every three months, as well as some of the schoolchildren returning for the summer. Vern was able to secure himself a ticket out of Repulse, and even though there wasn't room for me on this plane, my hope was rekindled that I too would be on my way soon. I knew with patience my chance would come. Vern would monitor the expedition's progress from the safety and relative comfort of Churchill for the remainder of our trek down the western shore of Hudson Bay.

The winds died down, and I helped Don reload the helicopter with supplies needed at the geologist camp. Don headed out that evening. I found myself the only Kabloona left in the village. I knew I may be here for a while yet. I went to talk with Father Rivoirre. I hoped he could make arrangements to get a pair of sealskin boots made for me. Agreeing to do so, he told me, "If you stay in the village for another week, you can join the co-op!" By then I found that truth funny enough to laugh at.

"I guess life in Repulse won't be so bad," I smiled. "I never dreamed Vern was so sincere when he gave me a one-way ticket to the Arctic."

A few days later as I was walking across the village, an Eskimo woman beckoned me to enter her home. I did, and she showed me a pair of boots—the ones I presumed the Father had asked her to make for me. They weren't what I'd expected, as only the lower half was sealskin, the rest being made of canvas material, and it had an excess of fancy embroidery I felt would look out of place on a voyageur. She spoke no English, and I knew very little Eskimo. At her prompting I tried one boot on, walked around in them, and smiled, expressing fabricated pleasure. Then, with my own grossly inept sign language, I made her understand that when the boots were finished the money would be waiting with Father Rivoirre and to bring my finished boots to him. I left her and went to see Father Rivoirre to tell him the boots weren't quite what I'd wanted, but to my utter confusion he met me on the slushy street holding up my boots—ones that looked like I'd expected.

"What a mess I'm in Father," I said, "I'm not sure, but I think I just ordered another pair of boots!" His frame shaking with laughter, he promised to straighten things out, but I was hoping I'd never run into that poor confused woman again!

Over three weeks after my return to Repulse from our failed attempt to cross the ice to the open waters of Chesterfield Inlet, Tagak came with news I was always delighted to hear but had learned not to rely on. "In the morning a flight may be landing, and you can leave." Tagak seemed certain this time. "We have no key to the city to give you," said Tagak, "so I made you this key ring out of walrus tusk." The carving was of an Arctic hare—a lucky rabbit! Perhaps it was, for at mid-day a Transair cargo plane glided onto the airstrip. Soon I'd be on my way to Chesterfield Inlet and my canoe trek homeward could resume in earnest.

I hadn't been crazy about being stranded in Repulse Bay for over three weeks, but what a blessing it ended up being. I'd come to the village as an outsider; I was leaving as a friend. While I hadn't become an expert in the Eskimo culture, I had certainly developed an understanding and appreciation for them that I'd never have developed by simply passing through the village. I'd also become more savvy as to what to expect from this land of ice and snow; it was reassuring that the Lord had provided this time of equipping before putting me back on the center stage of expedition travel. I'm not sure how one quantifies what might have happened, but I'm quite confident that my chances of survival improved immensely as a result of the time I'd spent traveling, hunting, and learning from the people of Repulse Bay.

The village of Repulse Bay, located just north of the Arctic Circle.

Tuktujuk and his family in traditional Eskimo dress.

A Taste of Open Water

"I can do everything through Him who gives me strength."
(Philippians 4:13)

Journal Excerpt: June 17, 1970

"My first time on the waters of Hudson Bay came at 6:00 p.m. today. It was a beautiful evening as we slid across the calm mercury colored sea...The thought of how stationary the pure white and sea green ice bergs were was shattered when at 10:00 p.m. the tide started to come in."

Fifteen minutes after the Transair cargo plane vibrated into the sky, I caught a glimpse of open water. Then thick clouds enveloped the plane and I could see nothing above or below, only the red tip of the wing and a maze of black threads looking like tar had been used to patch the wing quite frequently. We were scheduled to refuel at Coral Harbor before going on to Chesterfield Inlet, but with visibility and radio contact nonexistent, we could find neither village from the sky. We continued to head south, and after nearly five hours of flying blind, we caught a break in the clouds and landed at Rankin Inlet, a village located south of Chesterfield Inlet.

Rankin Inlet was not used to accommodating outsiders. The only place available to stay was a dilapidated old bunkhouse that looked like a converted sheep shed. Three other men were lodging there; covered with dirt, long hair, and the smell of cheap liquor. I didn't plan on hanging around long enough to learn their stories! It didn't appear the lumpy hard mattress would offer any more comfort than sleeping on a caribou hide and tundra rock. The walls were extremely thin, no more than the thickness of a single board separating room from room, and my warped door wouldn't close, prompting me to brace a rickety chair under it when I turned in for the night.

I was at the bay store when it opened in the morning. I hoped that the manager here would be as friendly and helpful as Henry Voisey had been at Repulse. After introducing myself, I asked if he knew of anything that was "Flying, walking, crawling, or swimming to Chesterfield Inlet," that I could catch a ride on. A young Eskimo boy stocking shelves said that maybe a hunter named Sik Sik would take me. The manager dispatched him to go find Sik Sik and invited me to wait at the store for him. An Eskimo came in looking around as if trying to find someone.

I asked, "Are you Sik Sik?"

He smiled and said, "No, I Eskimo," and everyone around me laughed. The bay manager explained to me that *sik sik* was also the Eskimo word meaning ground squirrel! I was embarrassed but joined their laughter.

Soon the real Sik Sik arrived. He was thin, weather worn, had black curly hair, no front teeth, and at a full six feet, he was the tallest Eskimo I'd met. His eyes were dark; the white no longer being white, but a murky brown. He spoke no English, although it seemed he could understand quite a lot. I studied his steady face and I trusted the man. Letting the bay manager handle the details, I agreed to buy our food and gas, and pay Sik Sik twenty-five dollars per day. He wanted to leave as soon as we could to take advantage of the weather. That was the kind of action I liked!

Within the hour, gear and gas were loaded on a two-wheeled trailer, and a tractor pulled us out of town to the shore ice and Sik Sik's canoe. His canoe made *Little Eric* look like a rowboat next to an ocean-going freighter. The gray beast was twenty-two feet long, a strong fifty-two inches at the beam; under its heavy canvas skin, it was ribbed every other inch, and solid planking strips ran the full length of its structure. I was guessing, but it had to weigh several hundred pounds. The canoe had a flat stern and was powered by a large outboard—the cover was so chipped and worn it was difficult to identify either the engine brand or horsepower. Tudlik, a younger Eskimo, would be joining us so Sik Sik would not be alone for the return journey. I was pleased to learn Tudlik spoke fairly good English.

Rankin was quite far from the actual bay and twenty miles from open water. With everything loaded, and the canoe tied to a komatik, we started out by snowmobile. Fifteen miles out of the village the Skidoo broke down, but by stealing a nut from here, a bolt from there, and rearranging the cogged rollers, Tudlik and Sik Sik revived the machine for about three more miles. Then it gave up. There was no repairing it. Pulling a twenty-four-foot komatik by hand that is loaded with a ton of supplies isn't enjoyable! For two hours and forty minutes, we floundered up to our knees in slush and water. Perhaps the experience wasn't entirely for naught as I learned to recognize different kinds of ice. Blue ice meant I'd be walking in a slippery two to three inches of water. Slushy gray ice meant safe walking with perhaps a few deep holes caused by exposed weeds, and dark ice meant six to eight inches of water and the probability of cold, wet knees. Wool helps retain warmth, but you must keep walking or your feet grow numb. Stopping for a rest, I dumped a quart of water out of my seal boots and put on dry wool socks, a ritual I had to repeat three times before our journey on foot was over. Every twenty minutes we stopped for a brief rest and a look at the area ahead. We spoke little, and there were no complaints; the Eskimos embrace the pains of travel as a way of life. Asking God for the strength to continue became as constant and natural as breathing.

When we finally trudged out of the slush and to water's edge, the sea looked calm and inviting, seductively calling to us, while hiding the cold brutal truth of its icy depths. For over thirty minutes, we rested and filled our bellies with Pilot Biscuits, corned beef, and warm tea. With a gull overhead and curious seals bobbing up and down in the water around us, we launched the canoe for my first time on the open waters of Hudson Bay.

The snowmobile that had broken down was given up as lost, to be engulfed by water when spring fully arrived, but to lose a valuable komatik was unthinkable to these men, so it too came aboard the mammoth canoe with us. It was lashed crosswise on the gunwale, giving us more the appearance of a seaplane than a canoe. We ferried it about a quarter mile to a rocky point where it would be cached, when we met with near disaster. As we prepared to land, the komatik slid off center, tipping the canoe dangerously to one side. With a final spurt of power from his outboard motor, Sik Sik wedged the canoe up onto the shore ice, stabilizing it enough so Tudlik and I could carefully get out and drag the weight of the heavy komatik back to a point of balance. We then pulled the komatik up onto the rock bank, where it would stay until it could be retrieved with the onset of next winter's snow.

It was a beautiful evening as we rode across the calm aqua sea. The silver clouds in the distance lined with gold by the low profile of the sun promised more good weather to come. My thoughts of how beautiful and calm Hudson Bay was changed when the tide came in. A light wind and the shifting tides meant rough water. The massive crowns of ice around us were now bobbing like toys in a bathtub, throwing spray three feet into the air; the waves themselves were three to four feet high. Each wave became a thrilling rollercoaster ride. Sik Sik turned the bow toward open water, as the loose ice moved in with the tide, narrowing the ribbon of water between the free-floating ice pans and the stationary shore ice. We scraped through what I refer to as sludge belts, where chunks of ice beat on the bottom of the canoe as if attempting to chip the bottom away. Once the floating sea ice separated us from the true shoreline, it would be hours before we could attempt landing. Hopefully, the weather would not worsen.

After over ten hours on open water, Tudlik said, "I see buildings."

"I don't see them," I replied. "In fact, I can hardly see shore!"

"You don't know where the buildings are," smiled Tudlik. We had reached the shore ice near Chesterfield Inlet. No one from the village saw us arrive as we had hoped, so we made tea and a smoky fire from some of our rubbish and wet vegetation—but still no one came.

"Ick," said Sik Sik, meaning *I'm cold* in his native tongue. But "Ick" was rather appropriate in English at that moment too, for with no snowmobile to carry us to the village, it meant more tugging of our overgrown canoe to drag it to safety. We slid the canoe rather easily over a quarter of a mile of ice. Tudlik and Sik Sik would listen carefully to the pops, pings, and bangs of the shifting flowage.

"Not far enough," Tudlik would say. And we would go on pulling, listening, pulling, listening until Sik Sik stood still for a long pause and smiled, "Eemah"—*yes, this is good.*

Once the canoe was safe, we still had a two-mile hike across a peninsula to the village. I found my sealskin boots to be quite slippery on the rocks, and the thin skin offered about as much protection from the hard stones as going barefoot. At the village, I met the area administrator, Robert Burns. "Welcome to the Vatican of the North," he said, and I soon found out why. The Anglican missionaries had long ago moved into Chesterfield, and the village now had a large church, a school, and a three-story hospital resembling an old schoolhouse. The sisters baked real bread, which my stomach found delightful. The fathers operated, what is beyond a doubt, one of our continent's north-ernmost chicken coops, housing fifteen to thirty laying hens. The main communication booster station between Churchill and the north was located here, and old movies, generally out of circulation in the States, were shown once a week.

It didn't take long to note the change between the industri-ous hunters of Repulse Bay and the population of Chesterfield Inlet. Here the Eskimos had reached a higher degree of civili-zation. I'd already noted in Rankin Inlet that being closer to *civilization* typically meant more access to alcohol and the need to lock up personal belongings—neither of those problems had been an issue at Repulse Bay. Chesterfield Inlet was located in an area of poor hunting; those that did hunt usually returned empty handed and were more or less forced to depend on wel-fare checks and to live (as some of the white men of the village said) as *mission rats.* Unfortunately, it seemed the Eskimos of Chesterfield Inlet would soon vanish if their life needs were not handed to them. It was reassuring to learn that Joe Issaluk and Kukliak were respected in the village as true hunters, since they were to make the dangerous journey north to Wager Bay with me; I wanted the best men available.

In addition to Issaluk, Kukliak, and me, our canoe carried nine ten-gallon drums of gas. All of it would be needed on the 250-mile trek north to Wager Bay where *Little Eric* was still stashed. We also carried food, a tent, and five guns—a total of at least a thousand pounds of gear. It was easy to see why this stout craft had been christened the freighter canoe. On the recommendation of some the Anglican fathers and the bay manager, Robert Burns, I prepared one pack as a survival kit. It contained a lifejacket, so it would float, an entire set of dry clothes, dry boots, and dry gloves wrapped in a waterproof bag, along with an emergency blanket and poncho, which could be used for shelter if necessary. At all times, I carried a watertight lighter and my compass, even though it was largely useless in areas this far north. These preparations were made primarily in case we capsized. Given the reality that the icy water offered only three to five minutes of survival time before one would be overcome with hypothermia, chances of ever using this pack were slim. We carried no life jackets other than the one stuffed in the survival pack. If something was to happen and we were going to survive, it would depend more on God's grace than our own actions.

The smooth surface of the sea reflected back images of huge castles of ice, as big as houses, some of which towered twenty feet above our heads. A look into the water showed them to be much deeper in the sea than what showed on top. My companions didn't like to venture too close to these mammoth towers of beauty, for with continued melting, the gigantic icebergs would sometimes rollover in the water, and there was always the danger of pieces weighing hundreds of pounds breaking free and sliding down on top of us. Compared to the icebergs, we were like a leaf floating in a puddle.

While it was energizing to be on the move again, I felt as if we might never progress beyond the confines of the Arctic. While I was anxious to recover *Little Eric,* it was agonizing to be heading north rather than south. I had to constantly remind myself that two thirds of the distance we'd eventually cover during the expedition was north of the Canadian border. I needed to be patient and trust the Lord's timing.

The farther north we went, the more ice we ran into. Maneuvering around free floating ice sometimes put us within arm's reach of the shore ice—and at other times over five miles out in the bay. We had reached one of our most distant points from shore when strong winds and the incoming tide overtook us. Almost instantly the waves swelled to a height of over six feet. We would teeter at the crest of one swell before racing wildly down the other side where for what seemed an eternity we would sit motionless is a canyon of water; then the process would start all over. We tried riding down the waves' surface at a forty-five-degree angle to prevent the bow from being buried in the water. We covered what gear we could with our canvas tent and my poncho, but riding low in the water with our heavy load, we began taking on water, forcing us to bail furiously or be swamped. We were drenched, cold, and in great danger. In my head, I understood that faith was a gift from God and not something that is mustered up from within us. I gained firsthand appreciation for that truth in this situation. As we struggled to survive, I found I wasn't praying in a desperate or panicked manner, nor did I doubt that God would hear my prayers; rather my prayers for God's presence were uttered with simple confidence. I knew I was in a situation beyond my control and likely would have panicked had God not given me the faith that the situation was not out of His control. We fought the waves for hours before we were able to work steadily toward shore (the rocky coast of Hudson Bay often prevents landing when necessary—especially if the tide is out) and land safely in a sheltered cove.

I walked around our stony shelter in search of some duck nests and eggs for our next meal. I stopped to peer into what I believed to be an old deserted cache used to store meat. It was covered over with caribou hide and a mound of rock. I thought it might have been used by a hunter and his family to keep meat fresh until they could pick it up on a return trip. But as I removed two of the rocks, I found it was an unmarked grave; the skull covered with lichens and long devoid of any flesh. A bit startled, I swallowed hard and replaced the rocks. Deep in my mind, I couldn't help but wonder who it was and how he or she had come to be buried here! Soon I uncovered the nests of two ducks and a gull. I raided the nests for nine brown-spotted green duck eggs, twice the size of chicken eggs—leaving some eggs in each nest. I left the smaller eggs of the gull, although Issaluk said they were edible too. Contrary to what many Americans tend to believe, Eskimos cook almost everything they eat; they do however seem to have a preference for rare meat, and as I found on this venture, a taste for extremely soft-boiled eggs. Fresh eggs were a nice addition to my diet, and I took one of the large eggs with eager anticipation. I cracked the egg on the rock, which was serving as our floor, table, and chair, and chipped away the shell exposing a fertilized egg! Issaluk and Kukliak seemed to enjoy the fertilized eggs; I found that with a pinch of salt, I too could swallow the iron-rich embryo.

A half mile from where we landed, there was a bright blue lake of melted snow. On its far side stood four shaggy caribou. I told Issaluk, "Gee, I'd like to get closer to them for some pictures." I expected them to react like the timid whitetail deer of Minnesota, and not having a telephoto lens, I had no expectation of ever getting close enough for really good pictures. The three of us walked inland until we were on the opposite side of the lake from the caribou. Issaluk had me crouch behind some rocks and said, "Stay here—get pictures." Then using our rolled maps and the butt of his gun for antlers, and with Kukliak squatting somewhat and converting his arms to horns, the two began a series of comical snorts, grunts, and whistles. Their crazy antics brought the curious caribou trotting around the lake, cautiously stopping to look and smell several times, but always prompted by their curiosity to come closer. In the meantime, I kept snapping pictures, having no idea that those curious caribou would shortly stand only three feet away. When my pictures were taken, we chased them off. "They ask for bullets," Issaluk grinned. Kukliak accommodated them a little while later, and we returned to camp with the hindquarters of a freshly killed caribou. Kukliak carried the meat like a packsack with a rope tied through the animal's legs and the carcass slung over his right shoulder and his head, adding still another layer of blood to the many dried layers already staining his jacket. When we reached camp, Issaluk immediately cut off some strips of steak and fried them. The wild meat was delicious, and between the three of us we ate six pounds or more in that one sitting!

The weather that returned with the next tide wasn't great, but we felt it safe enough to travel. We cached five drums of gasoline at this point, marking its location high up on a hill with a pyramid of rocks that my companions would be able to recognize from the bay. Between the gasoline we'd already used and this cache, we now traveled at least five hundred pounds lighter. We secured the caribou carcass across the bow of the canoe where the meat would be cured by the saltwater spray and the intense sun. I thought we would all die of laughter at the expression on Kukliak's face when a white-capped wave snatched his bent-barreled rifle from his hands and buried it in the depths of the sea. It was easy to see why all of their guns looked so abused and ancient, for Issaluk had brought along a well-oiled, polished shotgun, which after a few days of salt spray and blistering sun, now looked like a rusted antique.

As we inched nearer to Wager Bay, I told Issaluk he looked tired. "Not tired," he said, "worried—conditions not good; must wait, maybe long time before can cross Wager Bay." I too was worried, for the tales I'd heard of Wager Bay were legendary! It was a large inland body of water with a narrow neck that connected to Hudson Bay. When the tides were going one way and the wind blew from the other direction, crushing ice and powerful currents at its narrows could destroy even large fishing vessels. Supposedly many boats and hunters had gone down in these waters and others had fallen victim to polar bear. On our map, I showed Kukliak and Issaluk where I thought the supplies were located. After much discussion in their native tongue, Issaluk traced a line across the bay at a point quite a distance from the bottleneck we hoped to avoid. Together we all cast a doubting look at the water, at present too clogged with ice for us to venture a crossing. For now, we would camp on the south shore of Wager Bay and wait.

As we waited for a combination of Lipton instant soup, snow water, and caribou tongue to boil, Kukliak broke open the leg bone of the caribou we were packing, cracking it with a rock as if it were a nut, and offering me a piece of the pink marrow. With my body becoming conditioned to eating anything, I willingly took it and found the fine textured substance tasted like butter. All my life I've been a lean meat eater, cutting even the slightest trace of fat from beef, ham, or pork, but my body had different needs now, and I actually craved the soft juicy fat, which surrounded the caribou meat. The tongue of the caribou was a delicacy for my colleagues but wouldn't make my list of prized Arctic cuisine; it was tough as a piece of rubber and tasted something like chicken gizzard. Not that Churchill is known for its fine restaurants or cuisine, but I couldn't help but wonder what Vern might be eating as I struggled to chew and swallow a bite of caribou tongue.

We watched the bay carefully as the tide moved out to sea, carrying with it all the loose ice that blocked our path, but it wasn't until the very end of the outgoing tide that we began our crossing. "Fifteen minutes or we not make it," Issaluk bluntly stated. Within minutes large amounts of ice forced us nearer and nearer to the narrows we had started out hoping to avoid. Kukliak and I cleared away what ice we could with our paddles; Issaluk stood in back of the canoe intently watching as swirling paths of ice opened or closed for us. Midway across, we became trapped in a small lake encircled by turning ice pans—some fifty feet or more in width and weighing tons. The ice pans were moving with enough velocity to actually leave a wake like you'd expect to see behind your motorboat. Every twenty feet whirlpools were starting to develop as if the whole bay were going down a drain! They started small, but many of the rapidly turning funnels grew to be eight inches in diameter and appeared to over a yard deep; we could feel the tug on the canoe from many feet away and in many different directions at once. Without cutting the engine, Issaluk ran the canoe up on an ice pan, and while he held the running engine up off the ice, Kukliak and I leaped from the canoe, straining to keep its momentum until we had crossed the ice pan and were back in navigable water. On one ice pan crossing, Kukliak and I broke through thin ice up to our knees, instantly numbing our feet and lower legs. We stumbled with unsure footing as we heaved the heavy canoe back to open water, hitting the water and getting underway in one motion. "Please Lord," I prayed as we franticly battled to keep afloat and not be crushed to death. The crossing lasted a half hour—fifteen minutes longer than Issaluk thought we could survive—but it drained our bodies completely, both mentally and physically. The legendary Wager Bay had been crossed, but we would be back and we couldn't help but wonder what our return trip might be like.

Eventually, we landed on a small island to check our map and get our bearings. The area we were now in was as unfamiliar to Kukliak and Issaluk as it was to me. There were two places on the map that showed three small islands in a row, and two points jutting out from the nearby coast. One was north of where the *Little Eric* was in cache, the other south. We were at one of those locations now…the question was which one! By now I knew an Eskimo often takes a great deal of time in making a decision and I wasn't about to pressure them, but after two hours we still hadn't decided which island we were really on. As head of the expedition, right or wrong, I was going to have to weigh the facts and make that choice. With my minimal knowledge of topographical maps, I carefully looked once again at the two localities where we could be. The map showed the points at the northern most area to be quite high compared to the surrounding country, while those of the southern most location seemed to be about the same height as the surrounding land. Terribly unsure myself, I concluded we had to turn south, back toward Wager Bay. My decision met no conflict. I had already learned from living with the Eskimos that they would rarely, if ever, disagree with a kabloona. Unfortunately it had been engrained in them that white man knew better, and with their consenting *eemah* (yes) we turned south. All I could do was pray my decision was correct.

Standing in the bow of the bobbing canoe, Kukliak continually surveyed the shore; he said he might have seen the canoe. But with heat rising from the rocks, the distant sighting was too distorted to tell for sure. We were within three miles of the canoe before I could announce with a rejoicing heart, "Yes, that's it all right." A weight lifted off my shoulders as I realized we had found *Little Eric* and our cache of supplies. Now my only question was had they survived the severe weather and sometimes eighty mile per hour winds that had buffeted the area over the past month. "Praise the Lord," I said as we found *Little Eric* in one solid, undamaged piece. Tapping the smooth surface of the imitation birch bark finish and laughing at the feather-light weight of the fiberglass craft, Kukliak, Issaluk, and I immediately righted it, loaded our supplies, and headed across the ice toward Kukliak's canoe. *Little Eric* slid across the packed surface of the ice with hardly any effort, a fact which my Eskimo friends found fascinating. I was surprised to see Kukliak's canoe, which we had left sitting on a large ice pan some distance to the north, had now drifted to a point almost directly out from where we had retrieved *Little Eric*. We immediately tied a towline to *Little Eric*'s bow and headed along the bank hoping to reach Wager Bay before it was again choked with ice. We were too late and were forced to pull up on the snowy bank of an island for tea, biscuits, and a long wait for the ice jam to break up. It would be at least four or five hours before there was enough open water to venture another crossing.

Even in the Arctic, the sun is warm enough, at least when one is dry and appropriately dressed, to make one sleepy. With nothing but time on our hands, I lay back across a large rock to absorb the sun's warm rays. In such a relaxed position and state of mind, I was about to fall asleep when the tranquility was shattered. First, the birds became silent, and then the entire island started to tremble until it shook violently like an earth-quake; with a low thunder-like rumble, we watched enthralled and horrified as a fifteen- to twenty-foot high wall of ice on the bay side of the island cracked along a widening fault for the length of two football fields and fell, in slow motion, into the lapping waves below. It sent a salty spray high into the air, birth-ing a half a dozen tidal waves at least four to five feet high that were now racing across the cold blue water. Seals and walrus quickly abandoned the ice pans they'd been resting on as the massive waves approached. The same thought was on all our minds as we raced wildly down the hill—the canoes and our supplies! If the avalanche of ice and walls of water had broken them loose or crushed them beyond repair, we were destined to die, for our treeless island was without plentiful game and well separated from shore. It was with three very glad hearts that we pulled the slack ropes of our rocking canoes back up the bank. We stood only fifty feet from where the ice had plunged into the sea, and our choice of landing spots had meant the difference between survival and disaster! For now the excitement was over, but soon we would wrestle with Wager Bay once again.

Kukliak's antics attract distant caribou.

Polar Bear swimming in the chilly Arctic waters.

Hunting Big Game

"This is the day the LORD has made; let us rejoice and be glad in it." (Psalms 118:24)

Journal Excerpt: June 20, 1970

"Give an Eskimo a gun, spear, or rock and it seems he'll use it to kill any living creature fit to eat. One of my colleagues just shot a caribou. He brought back the bloody, hair and lichen covered hind quarters. We immediately cut off and fried some stripes of meat; from hoof to mouth in less than twenty minutes!"

Our second crossing of Wager Bay with its churning water and crushing ice floes awaited us. To face its unpredictable and unforgiving waters two times in a matter of days was a daunting challenge. However, our apprehensions melted away as we gazed out over Wager Bay from its northern shore. Call it circumstances, good timing, luck, or God's favor—unlike our last life-threatening passage, this time the water was flat, and we found rivers of water weaving between the ice pans. We made the crossing easily and safely, and we did indeed rejoice at our good fortune.

It was early morning on June 21 when we slid across the mirror-like waters to Wager Bay's southern side and prepared to make camp. Perhaps we had capitalized on the proverbial *calm before the storm* for as we were unloading to make camp we could see a dark belt of black clouds to the extreme north and east. If a storm was coming, we knew it would be better to travel while we could, and to rest later when overtaken by rough weather. So, tired as we were, we reloaded the canoes and continued south. We'd now been traveling for fifty-five straight hours without setting up camp. Most of that time so far out in the bay that we could not see land. Given that we were miles from shore, we precariously balanced our Coleman camp stove on the center thwart of the canoe and made tea from a kettle of snow we had taken on board before leaving our last campsite. Drinking warm tea every four hours or so, regardless of where one was, was more than the equivalent of an American coffee break. It was an essential need if one was to avoid chills and illness in this cold wet environment.

An Eskimo rarely travels to the point of exhaustion, so by shuffling our gear and piling up a stack of caribou hides, a bed was made in the center of the canoe so we could sleep one at a time while a rested man ran the outboard motor. The third party, seated in the bow of the canoe, helped keep at least one sleepy eye open for trouble. When it was my turn to rest, I propped my soggy boots up on a piece of the heavy tent canvas for added protection from the cold wooden ribs of the canoe. Kukliak patiently manned the makeshift vice-grip handle of the motor, and Issaluk kept watch from the bow. I was half lying and half sitting with my head pitched forward, nearly asleep when Kukliak gave a shrill whistle, and I turned to see what was happening. Kukliak was pointing excitedly ahead, but as I turned to look, I saw only a bare rock outcropping similar to those I had seen many times before. Then I realized that this fifty-foot jet-black object was a moving island of flesh—an enormous whale! At that instant, like a relief valve on a steam engine, there was a large puff and a vapor of water rose several yards into the air. We were within a few canoe lengths of the whale when it rolled under the sea. Its shiny back—at least five times the width of our canoe—rose higher and higher into the air until with a wave of its unbelievably large tail, it sank, leaving a tidal wave of turbulent water behind it.

In my mind, being in a twenty-foot canoe and meeting a fifty-foot long whale meant it was time to head for shore; instead, Issaluk handed me my camera and questioned, "Kabloona want good pictures?"

"Sure," I said as I thought to myself, *but I want to be around to see them!* Whispering a prayer and wishing we were headed for shore, I loaded up my camera. With Issaluk standing stoutly in the bow and with *Little Eric* still dragging behind our freighter canoe, we headed in the same direction as our submerged friend. We slowed to an idle and waited, with me almost hoping the magnificent beast wouldn't reappear. But six minutes later a distant spout showed us where he surfaced, and we were off chasing to within one hundred feet of him allowing me to get some excellent pictures. To see such a monstrous, free, graceful figure on the open water was thrilling. Again, the whale disappeared. With watchful eyes, we circled the area hoping to catch an additional look at our magnificent visitor. Unexpectedly, the whale surfaced so near our canoe that the water displaced by its enormous bulk pushed the canoe sideways. Energized by an adrenalin rush unlike any other I'd experienced, I snapped pictures in rapid succession. Everything was happening so fast. Within moments the whale's tale fin towered over the canoe like a mighty mast, and as it slapped the water, the entire canoe was drenched with the salty spray—including the camera I held in my hands. Throughout the trip, I had been so careful to protect the camera and keep the rolls of film I'd taken safe and dry in a watertight container. Now one of my most treasured rolls of film and perhaps the camera had been ruined. The whale disappeared in the depths of Hudson Bay. I spent the next hour painstakingly cleaning the camera and lens. The camera had been saved, but this day, there would be no good pictures.

I'd learned that each day in the Arctic brought its own beauty and burdens. Today was no different. We were running low on gasoline and couldn't locate our cache. We didn't have enough gasoline to comb the shore in search of our hidden fuel supply. So, landing on the shore ice and leaving Kukliak with the freighter canoe and outboard, Issaluk and I took *Little Eric* and paddled the shoreline in search of our fuel cache.

I'd paddled canoes on much rougher water than what Issaluk and I saw that day, but the canoe was hard to manage. I quickly determined that the high bow and stern on our replica voyageur canoe acted as mini-sails when buffeted by the bay winds. Although we said nothing to each other aloud, Issaluk and I could see in each other's eyes that we both felt the craft was unstable. We took *Little Eric* about five miles and concluded that the cache had to be further south, so we slowly made our way back to where we had left Kukliak

Kukliak said he had seen a polar bear while we were gone, making me wish I had volunteered to remain with the freighter canoe. My disappointment was short-lived. A half-hour later we spotted one of the huge yellow-white animals walking along the water's edge. He started to amble away at the sight of the canoe, his stomach moving out of sync with his legs, giving him a comical appearance as he lumbered along. Issaluk fired a shot into the ice near the bear hoping it would take to the sea. His plan worked, and we canoed to within ten feet for some good pictures as the bear paddled along, snorting at us through the water, making a sound much like that of a whale spouting. As I held my camera securely over the gunwale of the canoe, Issaluk would whistle at the bear causing it to turn its massive head toward us. Its large dark eyes were piercing, as I looked at him face to face through the lens of the camera. Then the black nose would go under the water snorting a warning for us to stay away. I clicked my pictures, and we left him to continue his journey to shore.

Given that we were now forced to stick closer to the shoreline in search of our supplies, we encountered much more ice. At one point I was awakened from my turn in our bobbing canoe bed to find that both canoes were barricaded in the middle of a canyon of ice pans. Kukliak pulled in *Little Eric's* towline as short as possible, and Issaluk and I got out of the canoe, jumping from ice pan to ice pan, and pushing them apart with our paddles, making a passage wide enough to pull the canoes through. On one occasion we were forced to pull the canoes out of the water and at least a hundred yards across the rough surface of a huge ice floe. After several hours of tedious and difficult travel our efforts paid off. We rounded a rocky point and found our lifeline, two more drums of gas.

Having found our cache, we knew we were getting close to Chesterfield Inlet. With our own meat supply running low and desiring to leave some meat with Issaluk's family before he continued his travels with me, we decided to interrupt our march south and headed to shore for some caribou hunting. We secured the canoes on a long rope so they could rise with the tide, and with the Eskimos packing their rifles and I my camera, we climbed the twelve-foot wall of ice along the shore for a brisk half-a-mile walk inland. Soon we spotted a small herd of caribou in the distance. Much to my surprise, my colleagues laid down their guns and started an impromptu theatrical show. They raised their arms above their heads, pranced around in circles, and continuously whistled and snorted loudly. Caribou are definitely not as easily spooked as the white tail deer in my home state of Minnesota. The curious and obviously nearsighted caribou soon approached to within fifty yards. They were so close I could clearly see their velvety antlers and the small frosty hairs around their muzzles. As I watched my colleagues, I could see little sport in their hunt. They simply picked up their rifles and approached the caribou as boldly as if they were cows grazing in a pasture. As I clicked my shutter, they downed one of the animals, causing the others to jump back and trot in circles. They shot another one, and the other two pranced away, only to return before the first two were even gutted, to meet the same fate.

As I took pictures of Kukliak and Issaluk cleaning the caribou, I concluded that if I ever ran a butcher shop I would import Eskimos to work for me. In less than an hour, they had all four caribou skinned, cleaned, and ready to pack out. Issaluk had used only a jack knife, and Kukliak my hunting knife. Issaluk and Kukliak were bloody from their armpits down. They wiped off what they could on the lichen or moss covered tundra. We each slid a carcass over our heads and around our shoulders and carried them like knapsacks the half mile to the canoes. With only one rest stop and a heavy load on our backs, Issaluk once lost his balance and went tumbling down. Fortunately he was not hurt. With several hundred pounds of meat divided between the two canoes, we gathered some fresh melted snow water for tea from the shore and took off.

We continued to see a lot of ice, but this time it wasn't pan ice. They were icebergs as big as houses, sticking twenty to thirty feet out of the water. By midnight the bad weather we had been trying to stay ahead of caught up with us and forced us to seek refuge on an island. We circled the island until we found a quiet cove on the leeward side, and there, where the ice was flat, we pulled the canoes up and lashed their thwarts together. We set up camp, and after our usual meal of tea, meat, and dry biscuits, we rested. I was exhausted and cold; I didn't even remove my parka before climbing into my sleeping bag.

My thoughts were tired and foggy, and I never lasted to the end of my silent prayer. One thinks of life and God differently when living in the wild. Tonight, I was safe and had food in my belly, and for that I was grateful

I slept warmly and deeply for thirteen hours, waking to a brilliant sun, blue sky, and a tranquil silver sea. I filled my lungs with the fresh clean air of the Arctic and lay on my back listening to the birds. As I lay there, I concluded that I loved this type of life and that any experience I lived to tell about was a good one. I was ready for another day.

As we carted things to the canoe, I threw a full ten-gallon drum of gasoline to Issaluk across an open ravine between two massive chunks of ice. It would have been awkward and treacherous to try jumping the crevasse with the added burden of eighty pounds of gasoline. The can slipped out of Issaluk's grasp, landed with a thud, then tumbled and fell with a splash into the water and out of sight under the massive and precariously perched icebergs that ringed the shoreline. We needed that gasoline, though it was obvious retrieving it was not going to be either easy or safe. The opening the drum had gone through was not much larger than the can and hanging over that opening was a massive jag of ice. I was aware that if the jutting edge of ice broke during our attempt to recover the barrel, we'd be crushed. I tied a bowstring knot in a wet rope and slipping it around my wrist, I handed Issaluk the other end. It was risky, but a task that had to be done, and I was the one most likely to fit through the hole. Cautiously I made my way down the rock as far as possible. Then sitting back on my heels I slid down into the hollow below the ice where the lap of the waves echoed and the smell of saltwater and seaweed permeated the air. I gathered slack in the rope to drop over a ledge to where our gas can was floating. Suddenly, I slipped on the weeds coating the granite and splashed into the cold water going beyond my boot tops before I felt the rope tighten as Issaluk attempted to halt my fall. The numbing saltwater again saturated my felt boot liners. More days of wet feet! I refocused on how I was going to get the gasoline drum back to the surface. I coiled the rope I had descended with and made a loop. I had no experience as a cowboy, so it took at least three tries before I successfully lassoed the bobbing barrel. I struggled to get the barrel over the first ledge; I could find no footing. Twice I managed to raise it half way out, only to slip and have it hit with a heavy thump on the rocks below. Each time the barrel fell, I hoped the vibrations would not cause the ceiling of ice to crash down. I stopped to recapture my breath. I could tell I was starting to show signs of hypothermia. Finally, after half a dozen more tries, Issaluk and Kukliak managed to pull the gasoline can and deadweight of my body up out of the depths of the ice cave and through an opening that had progressively gotten smaller as the iceberg leaned farther forward. While Issaluk finished loading, Kukliak made me tea and helped me slip into the comfort of some dry clothes and wool socks. He vigorously tried to rub life back into my cold feet, and to squeeze as much water as he could from my felt boot liners. Within an hour, I had recovered enough for us to continue our trek.

About midday, we started to have motor trouble. At times the engine ran as if at full throttle. Then it would slow to an uneven putter, give a desperate gasp, and die all together. Dumping some of the gas out, we could see a distinct line between the light orange gas and the clear surface of water. Somehow water had gotten into our gas tank! Draining the tank into an empty drum, Issaluk opened up a new one in hope of finding better fuel. The watery gas would be saved—as we'd likely need it.

Kukliak, who possessed the best eyes of the expedition, pointed out twelve walrus. Despite recent findings, which indicated that the walrus was supposedly not as dangerous as many

Eskimos believed, superstition made my colleagues approach these obese, brown-tusked animals with greater care than they had thus far done with either whale or bear. In the space of the next two hours, we saw at least sixty walrus, occasionally getting within twenty-five feet of them where the smell of the ice pans, painted brown with feces, saturated the air with a fishy smell. We finally found one lone bull basking on an ice pan. This is about the only way an Eskimo will hunt it for fear that when more than one of the enraged or frightened animals enters the water, they will be able to outmaneuver the canoe and perhaps tear it apart with their powerful tusks or well-padded bodies. The ivory was still a valuable prize to the natives. Issaluk and Kukliak wanted this one, so slowly we drifted in toward it, the engine idling in the event that the walrus should come after the canoe. Issaluk hit it with his first shot. The walrus' nearly two-ton body flopped violently into the water. It turned frantically trying to get up on the ice floe again. Issaluk fired a second shot. The walrus thrashed violently in the water, which was now a sea of red from the animal's blood. In the final throws of death, the walrus climbed up on the edge of the ice where Issaluk put the fatal bullet into the skull. We turned about quickly, approaching the frail corner of ice the walrus' lifeless form was stretched over. As we landed, the ice gave way, and the walrus slipped silently into the sea and sank like a piece of metal. It was lost, a fruitless and now useless kill. I felt badly about the hunt because of its outcome, but indeed found it strange that while a seal would float when shot in the water, providing it had winter fat, and a polar bear or whale would float when shot in the water, a well-padded walrus would sink immediately!

With a deafening crack, we rumbled over a jagged piece of ice, much like we had done when leaving Chesterfield Inlet to head north, but this time it was the canoe and not the ice that gave way. The boards across the back of the canoe were badly cracked, but fortunately not broken out. Shutting the engine off we paddled to the nearest ice floe large enough for us to pull the canoe up on. We removed the heavy engine, and with a knife and a file, Issaluk bore a hole through the cracked wood and through a brace, which had suffered no damage. We borrowed a nut, bolt, and wooden brace from *Little Eric* and made some makeshift repairs. After much talk, my friends seemed satisfied that the canoe would hold up, but for added assurance when they put the engine back on, they tied it in place with a set of double ropes that were anchored to the middle thwart of the freighter's heavy frame.

We estimated we would reach Chesterfield Inlet within the day. Now backed by good weather, hunting again became an important part of our activities. We stopped to stalk a small silver seal bobbing up and down in front of us. Issaluk loaded both his rifle and filled his shotgun with shorts. Without apparently taking much aim, Issaluk pinged away at the seal with the shotgun, shooting just close enough to make the curious fellow dive, only to surface and immediately be forced to dive again. This kept up for twelve or fifteen shots. Deciding the animal had been sufficiently deprived of an opportunity to catch its breath, Issaluk picked up his higher caliber rifle while the seal was under water one last time. It came up for a long breath, and with careful aim, the bullet smacked into the skull, killing the seal instantly, ruining only a minimal piece of the skin.

We went over to his prize, and Issaluk pulled the silver seal out of the water by its blunt hind flippers. Laying the bloody head to the outside of the canoe, he covered the shiny wet fur with his jacket. Sensing that I didn't understand why, he pointed at the sun. "No cover—get sun burned—turn yellow," he said.

As we re-entered duck country Issaluk handed me his shotgun and pointed at an approaching flock. I loaded, aimed, and much to Issaluk's and Kukliak's surprise—as well as my own—with the loud blast, a duck fell from the flock to the water below. "Miterk no good," said Issaluk in reference to my duck, "Wrong kind."

"What do you mean wrong kind?" I pressed rather disturbed that my trophy was being left behind.

"Too salty, tough," smiled Issaluk. "Boil him with rock for long time, then better to eat rock!" His comments made us all laugh. Jubilant, and by all means glad to be this far south, we soon sighted Chesterfield Inlet. We pulled the heavy canoes in only far enough for temporary safety and then walked into the village. We would return for them later with snowmobiles.

Rather glad to see someone his own age, I was immediately invited in for a cup of coffee by the young twenty-two-year-old bay manager, a Scotsman name John Wallace. "Ya might as well bunk here with me, Barry," he said. "You'll be stayin' in one of the oldest Hudson Bay houses still in the Arctic." Happy to have the company of an English-speaking person near my own age and always fascinated by the sound of a Scottish brogue, I willingly agreed.

After a beefsteak dinner and some restful conversation, plus a dozen well-sugared cups of coffee, John and I went to a cowboy movie being shown at the village's recreation center. For me the drum of hoof beats on the trail was a welcome change, and for John it was a heavenly evening, for I was soon to find out he was an ardent cowboy admirer. His favorite actors, movies, and most of the reading material in his home were about the American Western cowboy.

After the movie, John and I returned to his home for more coffee and conversation. Starting with cowboys, our discussion moved into such things as his coming from Scotland at the age of seventeen to work for the Bay Company. He was the youngest Hudson Bay manager in the North. We spoke of the importance of faith and dabbled into off-the-wall topics such as interpreting dreams and where animals go when they die. We ended our enjoyable evening by concluding that one couldn't die a natural death because, well, it just wasn't natural!

We'd found our cached supplies, we'd arrived safely in Chesterfield Inlet, my colleagues had been successful in providing food and other provisions for their families, I'd had an opportunity to speak English with someone my own age, and most importantly I was headed south. Life was good, and I had much to celebrate.

Pulling Little Eric onto an ice pan.

Hunting the silver seal.

By Trial and Error

"Who shall separate us from the love of Christ? Shall trouble
or hardship or persecution or famine or nakedness or danger or sword?...For I am convinced that neither death nor
life, neither angels nor demons, neither the present nor the
future, nor any powers, neither height nor depth, nor anything else in all creation, will be able to separate us from the
love of God that is in Christ Jesus our Lord."

(Romans 8:35, and 38–39)

Journal Excerpt: June 30, 1970

"We nearly capsized three times today—we would have except for our
make-shift outriggers. Yet, each time an outrigger hit the water gallons
of salty brine flooded the canoe. It was a tense, tiring and wet miserable day."

Bay Manager John Wallace allowed me to use the warmth
of his rustic home with its indoor tank of coveted
melted snow water to wash my clothes for the first time
in a little over two months; causing me to smell as well as look a
great deal like the original fur traders! The clothes half dried in
the wind and half freeze dried on his outdoor clothesline, which
was located a good eight feet above the ground to accommodate for winter snow levels. With my domestic chores done, my

thoughts turned to plans for the continued sojourn south. After our less than stellar first experience of actually canoeing on the open waters of Hudson Bay, I was anxious to get Issaluk's honest opinion of *Little Eric*'s suitability for Arctic travel. I wanted, and needed, him to understand that he and I were in this situation together, that I valued his expert opinion more than he needed input from a novice explorer like me. It was like pulling teeth, but finally he said what I'd previously seen in his eyes.

"Too tipsy—not make it to Churchill."

"Very well, Issaluk," I replied, "we will continue to tow *Little Eric* until we get off Hudson Bay and reach the river country." It was better to be safe then sorry, I thought, for our lives depended on our craft and how well we could handle it. *Little Eric* was a fine river canoe, but Hudson Bay was not a river.

We set our departure for the next day. John offered to help me pull together the supplies Issaluk and I would need to reach the village of Wale Cove. Like most Hudson Bay stores in this desolate area of the Arctic, his store carried little more than the bare essentials we needed with the exception of one luxury item he stocked in large quantities—Coca Cola. Nothing is happier than an Eskimo boy with a can of cola, and it seemed they consumed it by the gallons—probably not a good idea given their limited dental care. Upstairs the bay store resembled a fur post from an old movie, for it was here that stacked piles of sorted hides were stored before being shipped. The Eskimos had to rely solely on the opinion of the Hudson Bay manager to given them a fair price for their furs. I purchased two fresh caribou hides for bed mats. We returned to the lower level just in time for John to weigh in a twenty-six-pound lake trout one of the Eskimo men had just caught.

Using the Bay Company short wave radio, I tried getting a call through to Vern at Churchill, but was unable to contact him until late that evening. I briefed him on what had happened and informed him that *Little Eric* was under tow and that we'd be heading south—weather permitting—in the morning. Vern was delighted to hear that the canoe was still in one piece. "Roger. That's it from this end. Any more from your end?" I asked. Not hearing a response I signed off, "Roger. Okay then, this is Chesterfield Inlet over and out."

John said my stay had been short but worth celebrating. So we did, with two family-sized steaks, enough instant mashed potatoes for twelve servings, and an entire loaf of hot bread from the Anglican mission located at Chesterfield Inlet. After that both John and I headed to our beds—likely the last mattress I would enjoy for some time.

"You know, Barry," John said, "I'm gonna miss your company." The feeling, of course, was mutual.

I lay motionless for a while thinking back on the trip from Wager Bay. I recalled how my head had itched so horribly after confining my hair to my shrunken blue stocking cap night and day for endless days. I had to laugh when I thought of how the hair of my beard had tied in knots and been caked with salt from the windblown spray and how all my whiskers appeared to be growing to one side of my face due to the constant winds. My hands and feet were always wet and on the verge of cold, and my teeth felt mossy by the time our trek from Wager Bay was over. I vividly remembered the torture of enduring long hours of nearly motionless sitting. Tomorrow I was to return to all of that. In spite of my reflections, I realized I was anxious to get started. It seemed my only goal in life right now was to keep heading south.

Although morning arrived with better weather conditions than I had expected, I was about to receive news that would make me sick. Vern radioed early that morning, "After all the public relations we've done featuring *Little Eric* as a replica of an authentic voyageur canoe, I've decided it would not look good if reporters ever found out *Little Eric* was towed all the way to Churchill, so I want you to use *Little Eric,* even if it means a later arrival than we had set." I was both flabbergasted and frustrated. In essence he was suggesting that the expedition's appearance was more important than our safety! I was spitting angry. It took me a good two hours to settle down. I had to believe Vern didn't really know what a risk he was asking us to take. After all, he wasn't with us when we ventured out on the waters of Hudson Bay with the canoe. I would explore options for making *Little Eric* fit for Arctic travel, but I resolved in my heart that I would not commit Issaluk and myself to needless danger even if it meant getting crosswise with Vern as the expedition's primary sponsor.

I wasn't happy at the thought of another delay, or about the potential for putting my and Issaluk's lives on the line trying to cross the Hudson in a craft not fit for the task. I told Issaluk there had been a delay, and that Vern wanted us to use *Little Eric* if at all possible. His look left no doubt that he was concerned about this turn of events. I mentioned the possibility of using outriggers, an idea that I had long pondered for use on the bay. It was Lou Couviette, Northern Canadian Power Company's representative at Chesterfield Inlet, who made exploring outriggers a realistic possibility. A thin man with long silver hair, a stubbly face, and a fondness for cigarettes and liquor, Lou said, "I don't want to see you boys leaving here in that small canoe or you'll both die. If it's outriggers you need, I'll help you build them."

It was settled. Once *Little Eric* was equipped with outriggers Issaluk and I would leave Chesterfield Inlet with it alone— providing a trial run showed us both that it was safe. In the meantime, Issaluk was to keep repairing his freighter canoe, and if *Little Eric* was still unsafe we'd leave the village towing it behind. One way or the other, we'd leave Monday if fair weather prevailed.

We slid *Little Eric* to shore by the Northern Canadian Power Company (NCPC) garage. We propped it up on two sawhorses; Lou and I scratched our heads as to where to begin. After drawing a rough sketch of what we intended to do, Lou and I scrounged up some five gallon cans, sheets of Styrofoam (readily available in the village as it was used for insulation), a solid eight-foot two-by-four, a couple of barrel staves, and a limited amount of solder. We soldered two Styrofoam-filled barrels together, end to end, and used a barrel stave to fasten the rustic pontoon to one end of the board. We repeated the process, then bolted the two-by-four through the center thwart of the canoe and lashed it down with twenty-five feet of nylon rope. It appeared as if *Little Eric* had grown metallic wings.

We tried metal waste paper baskets, a gas funnel, and buckets as possible means of getting a pointed end on our blunt pontoons, but nothing proved satisfactory until Lou reverted to his geometry days and cut a cone shape from a roll of galvanized tin. It fit perfectly. The pointed end would help break the waves, and we weren't too concerned if it leaked or not as we'd left a hole for water to drain out. We were more concerned about the fact that we didn't have enough solder to tack both points securely in place.

"I've only got one idea left," said Lou, in his usual swear-studded vocabulary. "We've got some paint around here that contains silver nitrate. Why, with it and some lead, I think we can make our own homemade solder!" Rolling up the sleeves of his worn red and black wool shirt, he layered a generous portion of the thick paint in a small trough we had bent from the tin. Then with the heat of an old hand-pump blowtorch, he melted a bar of lead, added another coating of paint, and more lead. The result was a dark colored solder bar which at that moment we prized more than a bar of gold. It wasn't the sort of material a technician would care to use, requiring a great deal of heat to melt and sticking with only partial success. But our heavy hand-made solder worked well enough to tack the nose cones securely into position. To my eyes, the strange craft looked beautiful, and in my heart I felt a renewed confidence in it for bay travel. It was late by now and our testing of the craft would have to wait until morning.

The bright spot in this latest delay was that it gave me one more evening with my new friend, John. We made the most of it. We filled his little home with our loud singing, covering everything from TV theme songs and operas to cowboy ballads, and of course "They call the Wind Mariah," which by now had informally become the expedition's theme song. We rarely remembered all the words of the songs we sang, but that did not inhibit our enthusiasm or singing. At one point during the evening, John demonstrated a seldom seen talent. While lying on his back and raising his legs over his head, he used a match to light the natural gas that he pushed out in a prolonged fart. Amazingly, he could throw a blue flame over a foot. This guy, I thought, has been in the bush too long! Our philosophical discussions went on long into the night and covered a host of disconnected topics such as the future, what is important in life, where we'd like to travel, and what sort of person we'd like to marry.

I met the morning anxiously and couldn't help but smile at the crowd of Eskimos gathered to watch the unveiling of the creation Lou and I had made. Carefully we transported our winged monstrosity from the NCPC garage down to open water by the bay store. I invited Issaluk, who was laughing hysterically at our winged beast, to join me in the canoe. Standing in it, we rocked the craft violently. For me the conclusive test was when Issaluk and I both sat on one side of the canoe—outside the gunwale! *Eric* wouldn't tip! Perhaps this would work out.

We pushed out into the open water for an hour-long test. The canoe stayed afloat even though it was holding Issaluk, me, and two of Issaluk's friends. At every indication of tipping, one of the pontoons would slide effortlessly into the water preventing us from going over. There were some problems. When caught in the slightest of rough water, the splashing floats drenched the canoe, making for a great deal of bailing. With our wings extending nearly three feet on each side of the canoe, it was like trying to maneuver a ten-foot-wide boat through the ice floes. Despite these handicaps, Issaluk and I agreed we'd leave in the morning with *Little Eric*.

Vern called over the short wave radio again and was relieved to hear we were planning on using *Little Eric*.

Issaluk and I packed fifty pounds of food, mostly salt, sugar, flour, and tea, along with our packs and other supplies over a mile of barren rock and soft moss to our now odd-looking canoe. I took my place in the stern of the canoe, with no hat, an open wool shirt, and sweat trickling down my back. The breeze was comfortably mild. The sun was shining down through a cloudless sky. The tide, however, had left a rift of ice that blocked our departure; we found it impossible to leave the inlet until removing the outriggers and dragging them, the canoe, and our supplies across a quarter of a mile of ice to a point farther east where a narrow ribbon of water was open to the bay.

Given the trouble we had experienced trying to maneuver our wide craft through the ice during our trial run the previous day, Issaluk and I decided to try installing the floats upside down, giving us another four inches of clearance above the water. This made the canoe a bit tipsier. We carefully loaded it so the supplies rested low and toward the middle of the canoe.

As planned, we were departing in *Little Eric* and I trusted the craft, but I felt certain Issaluk still wasn't so keen about it. If that were true, I reasoned he would overcome those feelings when he got used to our new *Little Eric*. Issaluk's wife and half a dozen children were still visible on shoreline watching our preparations to leave. In my mind, comparing this departure to the one at Repulse, I found it strange and sad that Issaluk never gave his wife or children a goodbye kiss or even a wave as we began what was to be a several-month and several-thousand-mile trek. It was our intent that Issaluk would be my companion all the way to the Gulf of Mexico.

We soon found that even with an added four inches of clearance, our outriggers caused nearly constant problems when trying to maneuver around ice floes. I discovered that I could shift my weight enough to raise one outrigger safely over icy barriers; however, the racket of metal against ice rattling in our ears typically accompanied those gymnastics. Within an hour, we were through the ice field and splashing through small rhythmic waves on the open sea. The canoe took on a great deal of water, and with waves slopping against the pontoons, the stern man got drenched. Our attempt to build a splash shield for our supplies only resulted in rerouting the water that ran like a steady faucet off the canvas tarp and into the canoe. By the time we were six miles from the inlet, the wind, which seemed to be changing directions, had turned 180 degrees. We pulled up on an island to look at the sea beyond. From the top of the treeless island, the view was disheartening. The change in wind directions had shifted the ice pack, confronting us with a solid blockade as far as we could see.

Pointing to where we would need to head if we ventured to round the ice on its eastern side, Issaluk said, "If wind change—we gone." He was right and I knew it. If we were on the outside of those miles of floating ice pans when the wind changed, we would be pushed helplessly out toward the middle of the bay. In our slow little canoe, chances were we would never reach shore.

Giving in to the mandate of the wind, I helped Issaluk cache our supplies on the island and then we headed back to Chesterfield Inlet navigating a narrow channel of open water that was quickly closing. I was discouraged. My quest to move south had been slowed, and I was once again headed north. The water was rougher now and each soaking splash added to my chill. The emerald green water no longer looked friendly. With a light load and choppy waves, we had nearly tipped three times. Each time we were held upright by the floats, but each time we took on gallons of cold, salty water.

It was early evening by the time we made our way back into Chesterfield Inlet. I was feeling very dejected. "Ya know, Barry," said John, "in my gut I knew ya were comin' back for another cup of coffee." I couldn't help but smile, though I wasn't quite as happy about my return as John. In our cold, wet condition, Issaluk was more than willing to offer his opinion—no more attempts with *Little Eric*. We'd tow *Little Eric* at least to Eskimo Point with Issaluk's canoe, for it was larger, faster, and safer, all features that would allow us to go out farther from the shore and around the ice that blocked our way. I was in full agreement. Vern wasn't going to like it, but it wasn't his life on the line.

After warming up and changing into dry clothes, I walked through the village. A small Eskimo girl of about five years of age came up and tightly wrapped her hand around the two longest fingers of my right hand, while her little male friend took my left hand. I smiled back at their dark little faces and happy mischievous eyes. Then prompted by a lightened heart, I started to skip. I soon felt like the Pied Piper, for in no time at all I had six boys to my left, all attempting to skip at different speeds and to my right were four giggling girls. Down the rough gravel road of Main Street we skipped until nearing the bay store. I attempted to join the hands of the two children nearest me. But shaking them off wasn't that easy, for with young laughter they clung to my hands like glue. It had been a long time since I had connected with little children! It had been great fun and renewed my disposition. I returned to John's to bunk down, for in the morning the rough role of the voyageur would once again be mine.

The quiet evening slipped by, and I arose to listen to the honks of two V-formations of geese. At least on shore the cloudless sky let the warmth of the sun be felt. This, of course, was no guarantee it would be warm on the open water. The brisk wind was still coming in, so it seemed a great deal of ice trouble was in store for us the first few hours. Trying to tow *Little Eric* through such tight quarters would be senseless trouble and weighted with gas for the long stretch to Wale Cove, Issaluk could do without my added weight in the shallow waters near shore. It was agreed that with the outriggers still strapped to *Little Eric,* I was to depart alone in *Little Eric* and meet Issaluk at the cache we'd left on the island the day before. It would mean a solo venture of about ten miles.

John walked the mile and a half to *Little Eric* with me to bid me farewell again. I hoped I wouldn't be returning this time, and felt deep inside that this time we would not be turned back again. The ice offered protection from the wind, so staying to its leeward side when possible; I traveled in solitude down a line of quiet dark blue water. The gulls screeching and drifting overhead gave no directions, so it was with a sense of satisfaction and relief in my improved navigation talents that I landed on the right island near our cache several hours later.

As I approached, I found the water getting extremely shallow for the tide was going out. It made it impossible to continue the use of *Little Eric's* side-mounted four-horse engine even though it had a shallow draft. I shut it off and quickly started to paddle with full, forceful strokes. But with cross winds hitting the high bow and stern and the tide holding me back, my efforts seemed fruitless. A strong gust sent me charging toward a fourteen-foot wall of ice. I put the paddle into the water as far as possible but my strokes seemed powerless. Only the outrigger, which took a loud and damaging smack from the wall of the iceberg, saved me from ramming into the ice broadside. With the dented pontoon grating roughly up and down the side of the iceberg, I bobbed in the shallow water under a massive wall of ice. Wasting no time in moving from that uncomfortable position, I used the paddle as a pole and pushed the canoe backward until I could step out and pull it across the ice to a safe location near our cache.

Taking a chocolate bar John had included in our supplies as a special treat, I worked my way to the top of the island to watch for Issaluk and stare at the icebound water on the island's south side. When Issaluk arrived he had to land 150 feet from the island due to the low water and a good quarter of a mile from the cache. He secured his canoe with a bowline to a large rock exposed by the tide. We removed *Little Eric's* outriggers and simply discarded the pontoons we'd worked so hard and creatively on. We loaded our supplies into *Little Eric* and paddled our way around the island to where Issaluk had landed. En-route we scared up hundreds of ducks. It sounded like a large wave breaking on the shore when their feet and wings beat the water trying to escape us.

We moved our supplies to Issaluk's freighter canoe and rigged a towline for *Little Eric*. Once the tide came in, we moved slowly but steadily for an hour before encountering a solid barrier of ice. Issaluk climbed up on a huge dome-shaped mound of ice and after staring with squinted eyes through his monocular for several minutes said, "All ice, but not go back. Must move quickly." We headed through a little creek of open water barely wide enough for the canoes. *Little Eric* had been pulled in tight to the stern of Issaluk's freighter canoe, but we still found it nearly impossible to wind through this narrow opening. My heart quickened with the hope that we would make it. Issaluk spent half of his time outside the canoe pushing ice chunks out of our way. The ice scraped along both sides of the canoes like fingernails being pulled across a blackboard. At times we didn't have enough open water to paddle and simply placed our hands on the ice to guide the canoes along the narrow channel. After forty-five minutes of this, we emerged from the acres of jammed ice pans as victors!

The sighting of a large, beautiful, white swan and a close up encounter with a big silver seal momentarily brightened our day. But before long we had to force our way through two more barricades of ice, which almost stopped us.

Little Eric started to pull erratically behind us because it had taken on water. Issaluk pulled *Little Eric* up parallel with us, and while I held the gunwale of *Little Eric* with one hand, I continued to steer the outboard on our canoe with my other hand. Issaluk daringly crossed into *Little Eric* to bail it. This was far from being as simple as it might sound. It involved some real acrobatics on the rolling sea. We couldn't land at that time for we were traveling with only sky, ice, and open water before us. In less than an hour, *Little Eric* was floundering again. Issaluk had nearly gone in the drink last time, making us both apprehensive about risking a repeat of his boarding routine. This time, Issaluk tried a new maneuver and stood with one leg in each craft bailing with an empty oilcan from which he had removed the top with his hunting knife. Muscles in my arms were painfully cramping, but it was necessary to hang on to the gunwale for Issaluk's safety. I watched nervously as he checked out *Little Eric*. Soon he saw them; a series of spider-like cracks running along each side of the canoe for at least two feet. They were allowing a steady stream of water to seep in. With Issaluk continually bailing the canoe from his dangerous position, we headed toward an island still an hour away. If he couldn't bail fast enough, we'd have to cut *Little Eric* free. My aching arms would need to persevere for another hour.

Once we reached the island, we carried *Little Eric* to high ground, and in anticipation of the tide going out, we anchored Issaluk's canoe on the point of the little island, securing its bow-line to a big chunk of granite. With no supports in its thin fiber-glass skin, bouncing on the dense saltwater waves had caused the center area of *Little Eric*'s flat bottom to pucker sufficiently to cause the fiberglass along both sides to start separating. *Little Eric* was going to need some additional bracing to prevent the problem from recurring. We couldn't deal with the need for additional bracing at this point, but our supplies fortunately included a small fiberglass repair kit. The question was would it be enough given the amount of damage the canoe had already sustained. Issaluk and I started to sand the waxy surface of the canoe along the cracks. It was evident that the damp handful of sand paper we had wasn't enough to even remove the hardened glaze. We could patch the canoe, but it would be a poor patch at best. Using my toothbrush to mix up some resin to soak our two patches in, we then smoothed them on hoping they would hold. I packed the remaining resin in the cracks on the inside of the canoe. The artistic birch bark pattern that made the canoe look authentic was now broken by two long ugly patches, but just then appearances didn't matter. We both had only one concern. Would the patches stick and would they hold back water?

When we slid back into the water, the weather was good. Soon the island was out of sight behind us, and we bobbed silently along for more than two hours, listening only to the quiet whisper of the wind, the babbling sound of water displaced by the bow of our freighter, and the somewhat arrhythmic hum of Issaluk's outboard. We could see only light blue sky and the dark water. It was calm now, and being this far out in Hudson Bay, we hoped it would stay that way.

With the weather favoring us, we took turns guiding the canoe along as the sun settled to the lowest point I had seen since May. It sat like a glowing orange pumpkin on the horizon, offering no warmth, but casting rays almost parallel to the surface of the tranquil bay waters. It was impossible to look ahead and tell if we were coming to ice that might cause us to detour for miles, or if open water was ahead, to see the dangerous jagged blocks of ice at or below the surface was impossible. For our safety, we slowed to barely above idling speed. After a long day on the water, our clothing was damp. We were chilled to the bone and soon began looking for a place where we could stop. With fewer ice pans to land on, suitable drinking water was also becoming a problem when so far from shore, but because of the tides, we had no choice but to travel in the deeper water farther from shore.

This time an island was a long time coming, and it was with numb shaky hands that we finally tied up the canoes. Issaluk started the Coleman stove while I staggered on stiff rigid legs to a snow bank; with a tea-stained cup, I scooped our kettle full of soft crystalline snow. My insides felt cold and dead. We put the kettle on the small hissing blue flame, which seemed to take forever to melt the snow on this occasion. While we waited for the water to warm, both Issaluk and I stamped around flapping our arms out and around our own bodies in an effort to keep the shivers away. The damp cold was piercing.

To my surprise, Issaluk handed me a potent, syrupy, thick cup of coffee, rather than tea. "Drink first," he said. "Warm you quickly. Then tea—that keep you warm long time." We both followed his advice, finding as much comfort in holding the hot metal cups as in drinking the steaming liquid. It worked. We both avoided the chills and I felt much better. We would rest here for a while before resuming our travels.

Cutting another slab of inch-thick corned beef onto the hard patties we called biscuits; I unrolled a map of the area as we tried to pinpoint our position. If we were on the island the map pictured, we were about seven miles from Wale Cove. When we started traveling again, the shoreline was just a thin dark line in a purple horizon. We saw no signs of the village. The outboard gave a flurry of coughs and stopped. It was out of gas. We added the gas we had saved for the Coleman to the few drops remaining from our last drum of gasoline. We continued to the point where we expected to see Wale Cove, but found only miles of uninhabited, desolate, dark shoreline. Finally, we saw a dim light. It had to be Wale Cove. We were going to make it! There we would be able to replenish our supplies and do proper repairs to *Little Eric*.

We cautiously started toward the light. Still three miles from shore, the sound of splintering wood resounded in our ears. Both Issaluk and I were thrown forward when his heavy canoe arched up on a rock and slid down its side with a deafening, scraping sound. We didn't see the rock before or after we smashed in to it; we would need to stay alert as we worked our way toward the shoreline.

We discovered the inlet leading to the village was still ice locked, so we landed on a nearby point of land. It was several minutes before I could stand or walk with any degree of stability. But by the time we had unloaded and pulled the two canoes to safety, my body was warming. We bedded down for the night. Tonight it didn't seem to matter that I had only the thickness of my parka and sleeping bag between me and the rock I was resting on. I felt I should pray, but I was so exhausted my mind didn't want to function. I guess I simply said what I felt, "Lord, thanks for getting us safely this far."

It was after mid-morning the next morning when Issaluk and I finally stirred from a dead sleep and ventured outside to look at the campsite we had chosen at about 3:30 a.m. We had camped on a bare rocky point void of simple lichens or any other form of life. We were still three miles from Wale Cove but to walk there along the shore would double the distance. We settled down for some tea and gamish—an oatmeal-like mixture I had brought along in case of a food shortage.

"Maybe someone see tent and come," said Issaluk.

"I sure hope you're right," I replied.

We waited for an hour and no one showed. We decided to begin our long hike, but as we started packing our belongings into the tent, the putter of a Skidoo engine slowly winding around the water-covered ice reached our ears. A minute later the Skidoo was in sight, pulling an empty Komatik. They had seen us. It turned out to be Issaluk's nearly toothless brother-in-law, but teeth or not, he was a welcome sight! With his arrival, we went through another round of tea before heading to the village.

Wale Cove was comprised of a short string of plainly colored small plywood homes, much like I had seen at Repulse. Issaluk went to the home of his relatives, and I walked up to the small weathered mission building where I met Father Papion. "Sit and eat now," said the slightly built father with a very strong French accent. "Tell me of this adventure of yours." While enjoying some hot soup, I tried to explain what had thus far been my experiences. When I spoke of some of the things we had encountered on Hudson Bay, he gently nodded his head in understanding.

As we walked outside, Father Papion looked at the sky.

"You should rest now, but the winds will change soon. Perhaps you should move your canoes and supplies to the other side of the inlet so the ice does not block your way." I thanked him and went, seeking Issaluk to share the father's warning. Issaluk's brother-in-law took us back to our campsite, and we plotted our strategy to move the canoes and our supplies to other side of the cove. To accomplish our relocation, we needed to head back out to open water and enter the cove along its southern shoreline. Fighting wind and an excess of ice, we struggled to get to the open water, and once we did, we bounced roughly over the sharp waves.

Halfway across, *Little Eric* was a quarter full of water, and from what we could tell in the white-capped waves, our patches had given way. Skillfully, Issaluk maneuvered us between the ice pans until we found a place where we could pull the freighter canoe to safety. We headed back to Wale Cove skidding *Little Eric* by hand over the sea ice stretching between the village and us. The ice was covered with so much water that we practically floated our leaky burden the entire route to the village. The last one hundred feet between the shore and us was open water. Dumping the canoe before starting, we paddled at racing speed to shore, taking on water rapidly.

Wale Cove appeared to be a clean and industrious village, but I had no great hope of finding sandpaper or fiberglass in the village. My search for such uncommon supplies this far north led me to Al Wright, the area administrator. He was a big fellow, standing over six feet tall and of stout build. He had close-cropped hair, was smooth shaven, and had a deep dent in his forehead to the left of his right eye. Despite his leadership position, he didn't strike me as a businessman for some reason. Wright had been in this area over thirty years spending much of that time as a Royal Canadian Mounted Policeman. Invited to dine with his family, I learned that he was a collector of old guns and swords, and he had spent many years helping the Eskimos design and build canoes.

I explained our trouble to him, and he replied, "Sure, we can fix that. Myself, I'm partial to fiberglass—in fact, I'm building a glass boat in the garage right now." We portaged *Eric* up to the Wright's garage where he used an electric sander to take down the cracks properly, taking off the entire glazed surface.

"This canoe wasn't made for Hudson Bay, was it?" asked Wright as he smoothed on the first patch.

"It sure doesn't seem that way," I replied. "Why do you say that?"

"Well," he smiled, "for the bay, this canoe is built too narrow, too weak, too rounded on the bottom, and too top heavy—but it looks nice." He smiled. "I'd call this a suicide canoe," he continued. "At the last village I came from, a couple of young kabloonas like you ventured out on the bay in a canoe like this despite our warnings. They didn't get very far. When they brought in the bodies, we wrote 'suicide' on the inquest."

"Al," I said, "I'm not that hung up on using this canoe."

"I hope not," was all he said.

Father Papion came in laughing, "One of the Eskimos just asked whose toy you were fixing, Al."

I was glad Issaluk and I had already determined that if we were to successfully cross Hudson Bay, *Little Eric* needed to adopt a big brother craft, one of the Eskimo wide-stern canoes.

Issaluk and Barry stop for tea.

Looking over Hudson Bay.

Trapped in a Storm

"The disciples went and woke him, saying, 'Master, Master, we're going to drown!' He got up and rebuked the wind and the raging waters; the storm subsided, and all was calm."
(Luke 8:24)

Journal Excerpt: July 4, 1970

"Vicious waves leave no time for mistakes or accommodation of the weak. While I've learned to love Hudson Bay's forceful and untamed ways…one must respect her. Someone upstairs was caring for us in today's storm—the fact I'm here is testimony to that truth."

We circled around the first of three unnamed islands and continued along its leeward side until we found a small cove with calm water and easy access to the shore. The tide was going out, so we anchored the freighter canoe to some boulders and left *Little Eric* floating on the low tide. In for an apparently lengthy wait, we carted our teapot, stove, and hard tack to shore. "I think I'll name this 'Rubble Island,'" I told Issaluk as three-fourths of the exposed area was covered with hand-sized rocks. Mounting the steep rock-strewn ridge, we came to a flat grass-covered area about fifty yards wide. Then we ascended another rubble strip to the island top where we found a thin mile-long meadow.

Looking at the rolling waves, Issaluk said, "Maybe stay here long time—two, three days." Scooping our kettle full of snow, we sat waiting for it to boil so we could make tea. Mosquitoes were swarming around us. I killed eighteen feasting on my leg, through my jeans, with a single slap! The sun was warm, but to avoid the misery of the unrelenting pests, I faced the wind, tied my hood up tightly, and even put on gloves. After some tea and a dry biscuit coated with salty corned beef, we searched the entire island for a reserve of fresh water but we found none—only shallow stagnate pools filled with mosquito larvae. That was not encouraging. There wasn't much snow left on the island, and drinking water would quickly become a problem. As evening came and the angry waves appeared to be subsiding, we agreed to push on for the next island about five miles away hoping it might serve as a better camp if the weather pinned us down.

Arctic Tern screeched a warning from above when we pushed off from shore and headed back out into the bay, but we did not heed or understand their cry. The farther we moved away from the shelter of the island, the more we began to realize that the bay was much rougher than it had looked from our rubble-strewn roost. I held my breath waiting for *Little Eric* to split open again after watching it skyrocket over the ever-growing waves. We were battered and salt splattered, bouncing like a ping-pong ball from wave to wave, until we could again hide from the waves behind the next island. Once on shore, we stripped off our parkas to let them dry in the sun. Issaluk said, "This better place." We immediately found two good-sized holding ponds that were filled with fresh water from melted snow. On one side of the island was a circle of rocks nearly twenty feet in diameter. It had been the base for a huge skin tent used years ago when his people still traveled as nomadic hunters, Issaluk explained. Looking at it, he said one that large would have been used for games and community gatherings. I looked up to see some geese fly overhead and contemplated how comforting it was to know that there was food as well as water here, just in case our stay on the island was prolonged. While our five-mile trek over rough water had been a calculated risk, it was worth it. Issaluk was right that this was a better place.

We didn't dip our paddles back into Hudson Bay for several days. Finally, the high winds subsided. The sky was overcast but appeared to be clearing, and the bay was covered with no more than a steady pattern of ripples. We waited for hours and conditions did not change. It was time to continue our trek south. An hour after we started, the ripples slowly morphed into waves that were short and choppy, which meant an excess of splashing as the canoe rose over the crest of one wave and slammed into the next one. The jolt of hitting wave after wave of the concrete hard saltwater was actually painful, penetrating every bone in my body. An hour later, we were in big trouble. A furious storm hit. The sustained force of the wind was tremendous; wind gusts were of tornadic proportion. Within minutes arching waves of gargantuan size made any attempt at returning to the island a suicidal option. We knew, because we had tried. We swung out on a wide circular path to bank into the waves gently, but the force of the wind made it impossible. Three times we tried. Each time we ended up tipping the canoe dangerously on its side where one wave blown out of rhythm by the wind would have thrown us into the icy water.

I couldn't help but remember the recurring nightmare I'd had about capsizing in Hudson Bay before leaving on the expedition. We hunched down low and to the center of the canoe to stabilize it and tried to escape the spray that flew several feet above the canoe and rained down on us until our heavy jackets were saturated and clung uncomfortably to our bodies.

We made a mistake by leaving the island but that was behind us. Every moment we now faced was on the thin border between survival and death. We had to bail constantly. We knew we were running low on gas and that without the power of the outboard to keep us moving forward at a manageable angle to the waves, our chances of battling the high, rolling banks of water were slim. Issaluk crouched on his knees, trying to empty part of a gasoline drum into the outboard's gas can, spilling as much on the floor and him as he got into the container. We prayed no water would enter the gas can or foul a plug; to our relief, the noisy engine kept sputtering.

After what seemed like an eternity, the storm hadn't lost any of its savage punch. The gale became more forceful, bunching the short, choppy waves into mountainous curls like I'd seen people use for surfing. Thundering with a deep roar, the sea would bulge as high as eight feet above our canoe and then would fall with a powerful rumble toward the stern. Looking back, all I could see was a concave wall of emerald green racing at us from behind and a thinner curl of water arched over our heads. *Little Eric,* still tied to our canoe by a towline, would fly over a wave, its entire twenty foot length breaking contact with the water, and then it would fall with a smack, muffled only by the growl of the waves. I pulled my knife from its sheath on my hip and kept it handy, prepared to cut *Little Eric* loose in the event that it capsized or appeared it might drag us down. What may have been only seconds seemed like minutes; sandwiched between two walls of water, we seemed to sit motionless, with no sight of land, only to be raised to the summit of another wave; again slammed harshly into the sea and forced to race down its face until trapped in another trough between waves. Despite our motorized power, the heavy freighter canoe barely made the crest of some of the towering waves, and from this perch, where we momentarily slowed, we looked ahead for shallows and rocks although I'm not sure what we could have done to avoid them. It was hard to estimate the damage we were sustaining from this relentless hammering. We knew some things had been swept overboard, and a quick inventory revealed that Issaluk's seat had broken loose and was gone. We heard the crisp *ping* of three canoe ribs that had cracked or broken loose from the hull, and our most buoyant pack—our survival pack—was nowhere to be seen. It was three and a half hours before the storm subsided and our exhausted bodies found relief. As we moved into the safety of an ice pack, which cut the energy of the remaining waves to a lulling rocking motion, I closed my eyes and thanked the Creator for another day of life. All I could mutter was, "Bless you, Father—thank you, Lord." For us the storm waters hadn't been stilled, but our spirits had been at peace; perhaps that unexplainable calm had given us the necessary faith and strength to endure the storm. We were alive, and we knew God was good. Storms are a fearful reminder that we need to rely on one greater than ourselves.

"Ya know, Issaluk," I said after a long stretch of silence, "there's always something to be happy about. This storm has driven us south!" Indeed it had—by nearly 150 miles. By early morning, we beached the canoe on the banks near Eskimo Point. Issaluk planned to stay with some relatives that lived there, and with little spring left in my step, I dragged myself up to the government staff house where Vern Schield was staying. Vern had flown from Churchill into Eskimo Point to do some film documentary of the expedition during the two-hundred-mile trek from Eskimo Point to Churchill. Vern was elated to see us, but Issaluk and I were tired and hungry after having spent the last fourteen straight hours on rough water. Our conversation was somewhat sparse, despite Vern's enthusiasm to know all about the trip and the storm we'd faced on the open waters of Hudson Bay.

The next few days were spent largely catching up on rest, getting familiar with the village, and repairing the damage *Little Eric* and Issaluk's canoe had sustained in the storms we'd encountered. Eskimo Point, coming from the north as Issaluk and I had, was the last Eskimo village on Hudson Bay. It was nearly four times larger, better equipped with power, and had a more dependable air strip than other villages I'd been in, yet the flat-roofed plywood homes, the sight of both native and more modern garb being worn, and the fascination the village children had with my whiskers and blue eyes were familiar village sights.

Little Eric, a fiberglass replica of the North canoe used by Hudson Bay fur traders, was a large canoe by most standards— twenty feet long, forty-one inches wide, over eighteen inches deep, and weighing approximately 165 pounds—but it was a river canoe, not a Hudson Bay freighter. After flying it all the way to the Arctic, *Little Eric* was destined to be towed to York Factory and the gateway of the rivers that flowed into Hudson Bay. *Little Eric*'s replica birch bark hull was picturesque, but it wasn't durable enough to handle the pounding it had taken on Hudson Bay. Along the underside of the canoe, webs of hairline cracks punctuated by larger tears had put *Little Eric* at risk of sinking. To avoid the puckering of the canoe's center as it bounced on the unforgiving waves, we would need to add bracing. We ran a rough two-by-six board the length of the canoe, using an axe and plane to ensure a tight fit in the bow and stern. Boring a drill hole in the thwarts and seats using my sharp knife as a counter sinker, we put in four braces, which held the plank tight to the bottom of the canoe. Hopefully our efforts would keep it from additional buckling and cracking.

With the canoes repaired, our supplies replenished, and the weather clearing, we were ready to make the push from Eskimo Point to Churchill. Vern had secured the services of another freighter canoe and as a guide had found Oovinick, an older Eskimo who for reasons I never learned simply preferred to be called Gibbs. Now we encountered a different kind of problem—one might say a civilized problem. Our departure was delayed for over two hours while we searched for Issaluk among his friends. I'm not sure if we eventually found him or if he found us, but by the time we finally connected, it was obvious that he was quite drunk. Liquor had been a rare commodity at both Repulse and Chesterfield, but at Rankin Inlet and here at Eskimo Point, the alcohol flowed abundantly. After some robust coffee and some additional time to sober up, Issaluk was walking semi-straight and insisted he was ready to travel. As it often does to folks who over indulge, the liquor made Issaluk more talkative and demanding than his usual quiet nature. When he said he was ready to travel, we shouldn't have listened to him. When he went to pull the starter rope on his outboard, he failed to shut the throttle down; as the canoe lurched forward, Issaluk fell off his rubbery legs into the shallow shore water. The cold sobering water barely had time to splash before he rapidly crawled back into the canoe and instinctively started to remove and wring out his clothes.

"Thank God, we weren't in deep water," I told Vern.

"Bet he's sober now," Vern grinned.

I gave Issaluk my extra pair of dry socks and boot liners as well as a pair of gloves. Gibbs gave him a dry pair of pants. With the incident behind us, we traveled straight out to sea for over an hour before catching up to a drifting continent of ice. Here Issaluk and I were to relive our travels: drinking tea, sleeping, pulling up the canoes, hunting, and navigating the ice, but after only a few staged photo shots, the sun refused to cooperate and a soupy fog started to settle in. We headed for shore.

Gibbs was an interesting man. He was fifty-seven years old, a ripe age for an Eskimo, given that only a limited number lived into their sixties, and because of his years of experience in help-ing the early Mounties, he spoke excellent English. He lived as a boy in an igloo, which had as much as a twelve-foot ceiling. In order to work on it, the Komatik had been used as a ladder. "In 1957 some still use igloo as home, but no one now," said Gibbs. I knew the culture of these people had been changing rapidly, but I couldn't imagine the shock it must have been for them to move from a temporary home of snow to an oil-heated, station-ary home of wood with electric diesel-powered lights. With a smile Gibbs added, "We have indoor toilet in igloo before you people." I gathered from what he said, it consisted of merely using a part of the igloo floor as a bathroom. "Clean Eskimo build new igloo every two month, and dirty man use same igloo all winter," he continued.

The stories Gibbs had to tell were interesting, numerous, and never ending. He told me of a hunt he had once been on during this time of year. Fog and bad weather had prevented his travels and blown all the ice far out to sea; on shore he could find no water and at sea no new ice—meaning the old ice was permeated with salt, so he had gone through the torture of four days without water. "Throat was dry," he recounted. And show-ing me two rusted five-gallon water cans he had placed in the canoe, he added, "Never travel without water no more."

The distance we covered the next day was limited. We posed for the pictures Vern had failed to get the day before. Vern directed us. "Turn this way and now that way" or "Paddle now, don't paddle" or "Pour some tea—now eat a cracker." I felt like some out-of-place movie star. Judging from his smile and amused laugh, I'm sure Issaluk, despite his cooperation, regarded the whole thing as some silly kabloona game that wasted perfectly good traveling time. Vern filmed and clicked countless pictures for two hours. As we left the ice, I got a good look at two netserk or silver seals, the last ones I thought I'd probably ever see outside the confinement of a zoo.

In striking contrast to what Issaluk and I had been dealing with, the bay was smooth. That was good. However, we now had other troubles. Issaluk had developed a sore throat and a stomachache that made him double up in pain, and his condition was getting worse. Deciding it was more important for Issaluk to get some rest than for us to put on miles, we landed at a high point on the mainland that Gibbs said had been used as a campsite for longer than he could remember.

The land was different now. For the first time since Repulse, the shore was not one of rolling granite hills, but it was flat as far as I could see. It was covered with green grasses that were knee high and thousands of delicate yellow and white flowers. The campsite was strewn with old kettles, teapots, empty gasoline barrels, and lichen-spotted bones including the horn of a musk ox and a polar bear skull. Non-biodegradable garbage covered the ground, making the site appear to be more of a garbage dump than a place to camp. How unfortunate, I thought, that we'd introduced cans and plastics into a culture that traditionally used only natural materials but never educated them on the importance of protecting the environment. Teaching the Eskimos how to properly collect and dispose of garbage was an obvious need in the villages I'd visited, but this was the first time I'd encountered such an obvious problem on the trail. It broke my heart to see the pristine Arctic area cluttered with manmade waste.

After camp was set up and Issaluk was resting, Vern and I went for a walk. About a hundred yards from camp, I saw a long thin object leaning against a rock. Its five-foot height made it seem out of place in this treeless plain. We had discovered an old flintlock rifle—still fully intact, leaning against a rock. The stock was covered with brightly colored orange and pear-green lichens, and the thin ramrod was still fastened to the barrel. I removed my hunting knife and carefully flaked off some of the rust on the metal plate above the trigger and below the hammer. Soon we could make out the inscription: "*Hudson Bay Co.—Made in England 1869.*" Vern and I were in awe at our find. As we carried our trophy back to camp, Vern said, "This goes in the museum," referring to a museum he'd founded to house the historic, interesting, and sometimes eclectic things he'd collected on his world travels.

We burst into camp and shared our find with Gibbs. "That gun's been laying there for years," Gibbs stated rather matter of fact and devoid on any of our excitement.

"Why on earth hasn't anyone ever picked this up before?" Vern questioned.

Coming from a world of different values, Gibbs replied, "Why would they? It doesn't work."

Indeed it didn't, but it was with great pleasure that we added it to the canoe's load. Vern and I returned to the site where we'd found it and double-checked to make sure the gun was not from a grave, in which case we did not feel we would be able to take it along. There were no graves at this open campsite, so we felt all right claiming the gun as our own. I couldn't help but wonder how it had arrived at that particular location and what had happened to the original owner. The Arctic has a way of leaving many stories incomplete or untold. This was one of them.

It was undoubtedly Issaluk's fall in the bay that had started all this, and his raspy breathing made me fear he was on the brink of severe pneumonia. Boiling up some strong tea and a hearty portion of soup broth, we tried filling Issaluk full of hot liquid. He was almost too weak to eat. We put the Coleman stove in the tent; the small blue flame of the burner kept the tent warm. Digging deep into my first aid box, I dug out the strongest antibiotic I carried—something my hometown doctor had prescribed for me to bring along in case I got dangerously ill. Issaluk was not used to medication, and I surely didn't know what his reaction to the capsule would be. By now he was so weak and ill that we feared we might lose him if we didn't do something. It seemed our options were limited, so I gave Issaluk one of the prescription-strength antibiotics, and we left him in the warm tent where he could continue to sleep.

If Issaluk was up to it, we wanted to leave in the morning as soon as the tide was in. One primary motivation was to get Issaluk nearer to a hospital should he need one. But the morning covered us with a thick fog making it impossible to see the canoes, which were a mere twenty-five yards away. The fog made our clothes feel uncomfortably damp. The winds pushed heavy, dark thunderclouds across the sky, and we could hear rolling white breakers slapping the sandy shore. We definitely couldn't leave, which meant at least a twelve-hour wait until the next tide was in.

Issaluk wasn't doing well, but his fever seemed to be dropping. I gave him the previous day's regime of tea, soup, antibiotics, rest, and a warm tent. The weather changed back and forth between stormy and clear. This game with the weather went on all day until a rough-water tide flooded the coastal flats again but offered no chance for escape. Our next try could not be until morning, so we told ourselves it was a good chance to get caught up on our sleep, even though we were no longer tired. The weather is king in the Arctic—one does what it dictates. Who knew how long it would keep us pinned here. I decided to take advantage of the down time to clean and re-arrange my pack. From a waterproof container I carried to protect my rolls of film, I pulled out a Saran-wrapped treasure. Before leaving on the expedition, I'd seen a picture in a Christian magazine. It depicted a young man fighting gale force winds from the helm of a boat; Christ stood behind him with His hand on the young man's shoulder. For some reason I'd cut the picture from the magazine, had carefully wrapped it in Saran Wrap to protect it, and had packed it all this way—now as I looked at it, I was overcome with emotion and sobbed. The artist hadn't known it when that picture was painted, but I knew that young man represented me. I had indeed felt His hand on my shoulder.

Our dishes and bodies seldom got washed on the trail. Fresh water was limited, and the weather was consistently too cold for even wet hands to be a comfortable or wise option. The babbling stream at this location, however, gave me an excellent chance to scrub our kettles and bathe myself for first time in over a month and a half. In the salt spray of Hudson Bay, one never had a good hair day, and with my scraggly red beard long enough to brush my chest, I suspect I looked like a voyageur. Out of necessity, my lack of hygiene while on the trail probably made me smell like one too!

As we waited for the weather to settle down and for Issaluk's strength to return, I urged Gibbs into another story session. He said he had spent thirty years with the Royal Canadian Mounted Police force during which time he ran a four-hundred-mile postal route from Churchill to Chesterfield Inlet using a komatik and fourteen dogs. "Carry twelve bags full only of letters," said Gibbs. "No boxes or anything else, just letters." He explained that all parcels to the villages had to wait for the ship, which came only once a year. Moving on to another story, he told me that only ten years before, he was attacked by a walrus; it put four holes in his canoe with its tusks, and had it not been for a nearby ice floe and the fact that he had a nine horsepower engine, he would have been lost. "Not like walrus," he said. I could understand why. I told him of my close encounter with a fifty-foot whale near Wager Bay. Gibbs shared that the last time he had been on the stretch of coast between Eskimo Point and

Churchill—where we now were—he had seen twenty-five orcas or killer whales. I swallowed my tea in a gulp, wondering if they were still around.

When Issaluk's health, good weather, and the tide all aligned favorably, we were able to move out. We began jolting across waves that were as thick as they were high, but soon the sea grew calmer and my clothes began to dry in the sunshine and breeze. For the first time in weeks, I was dry and warm from my socks on up. Things were changing. Even though we were still north of the tree line, as we made our way toward shore to set up camp, we found piles of bleached driftwood. This evening we would have a warm fire. As we searched the shoreline for wood, we found a log. Struck with an inspiration, Gibbs, Issaluk, and I lugged, tugged, and rolled the heavy monster up an incline to our camp. Struggling together we erected our own tree, a twenty-foot branchless piece of driftwood with an eight-inch butt. It was hard work upending it, and to hold it upright, we had to place numerous forty-pound rocks at its base. Together we had erected the only "tree" between the real tree line that starts just north of Churchill and Eskimo Point. As we found the next day, its straight branchless frame and height made it a landmark one could see from miles away.

This place lacked the freshwater stream that had cut across our last campsite. People seem to forget that the Arctic area is quite arid and that the tundra can challenge travelers with thirst much as a desert would. On this site we found only two quarts of brown, stagnate water filled with mosquito larvae. Stripping off my T-shirt, I used it as a strainer to "clean" the water; we brought the water to an intense boil and then let it sit until it had cooled. Without hesitation we made tea and were simply grateful for something to drink.

The weather continued to hold, allowing us to make good time. About two hours north of Churchill, we noted two changes on the horizon. First, the shoreline took on a new appearance; against the blue skyline one could see the jagged shape of a forest of skinny trees. What an interesting forest! The cold northwest winds stunted the growth on the north side of the trees—giving the entire forest the appearance of Christmas trees that had been split in half. Virtually every tree had branches on only the south-facing side of the spindly trunk. The second thing one noted on the horizon was what appeared to be a small tower. It was actually the huge grain elevator located in Churchill's harbor.

We slid unnoticed into the Churchill River, past the old stone fort that for over a century had been standing guard over those that traveled her waters. We made our way past the shadow of the grain elevator until finding a spot where we felt we could beach the canoes. The shoreline was far from park-like and offered neither shade nor a sandy place to land. Once the canoes were secured, my mind was focused on a square little historic building on a side street of the city. It was a chapel that had been used by early Arctic explorers and those that had come after them. Men that had wrestled with the Arctic long before I was born had gone to that chapel to ask for and give thanks for safe passage; being of kindred spirit, I knew I needed to make my way to that sacred building. I had someone I needed to thank.

Barry determines it's safer to tow Little Eric.

Vern admires the flintlock rifle.

From Churchill to York Factory

"But those who hope in the LORD will renew their strength. They will soar on wings like eagles; they will run and not grow weary, they will walk and not be faint." (Isaiah 40:31)

Journal Excerpt: July 17, 1970

"Hudson Bay both made me curse and pray for my very life. I often wished I were an artist so I could capture her beauty. I couldn't take my eyes off her as we headed up the Hayes River. I felt as if I were telling an old friend good-bye for the last time."

O ur stay in Churchill would be a short but welcome break from the rigors of the trail. Issaluk and Gibbs were able to stay with some relatives, and Vern had secured rooms for him and me at the Churchill Hotel. The accommodations were basic, but given the weeks I'd spent sleeping on a caribou hide spread over bare rock, even a well used single bed was a real treat. The hot bath and shower was my first in nearly nine weeks! I cleaned up well but wondered if they'd ever be able to remove the ring of grime I left behind. Being in Churchill also provided me with the opportunity to contact my loved ones by radiophone. Such calls need to go through an operator and you cannot hear the actual voices of ones you've called. At least I was able to let them know I was safe. It was nice to hear the operator say, "They love you and want you to know they pray for you daily," but such messages don't seem as personal when being relayed through a third party.

The Eskimo family is a close-knit unit, which usually travels together. The trek Issaluk and I had completed from Wager Bay to Churchill had already taken him away from his wife and seven children for longer than at any other time in his life. He would often look at our map and the short distance we'd gone and then he'd ask me to show him how far we had yet to go before reaching the Gulf of Mexico. It didn't come as a total shock when Issaluk shared, "I quit—I go home now." I couldn't find it in my heart to be angry at him for quitting. Issaluk had been an excellent guide and a good travel companion. I likely owed my life to his skill and experience. I could understand his desire to go home, but I was not happy at the prospect of losing him. Vern was a bit more upset. He feared that all the expedition publicity about an Eskimo and an American crossing North America from north to south in a canoe might be at jeopardy.

There were only two hundred more miles of Hudson Bay left to traverse before reaching the river country traveled by the early voyageurs, but those remaining miles could not be taken lightly. Nelson's Shoal, constituting some of the bay's largest tidal flats, was in this area, as well as Marshy Point, which I knew for a fact to be the grave of several inexperienced canoeists. By now I'd logged 1,200 miles on the bay, but I had no intention of taking that final stretch by myself or with an inexperienced canoeist. As Vern and I started to ask around, we found that the village was nearly void of men who wanted to travel that section of the coast because it was known to be so treacherous. Everyone we confronted met us with the same reply, "Not me—perhaps you'd better talk to Jimmy Spence. He's the only one who really knows that shoreline. You need to dig up Jimmy

Spence." The name Jimmy Spence was referred to me so many times, he began to sound like some mythical character I'd never really find.

Jimmy Spence's humble home was located on the outskirts of the village, its weathered boards worn smooth by the relentless winds. In front of the house in an old wooden chair sat Jimmy Spence. I smiled. It did appear as if someone had "dug up" Jimmy Spence! He reminded me of a character you'd envision when reading Hemingway's novel *The Old Man and the Sea*. Spence was seventy years old, but his burly body was as sound as the rock we stood on. His raspy voice sounded alert, cautious, and self-confident. He was a half-breed—likely Cree and French although he wasn't too certain. His bald head was fringed with unkempt hairs that were outnumbered by the long curly hairs that grew from his ears or protruded from his nostrils. His eyes had acquired a natural squint from years of looking into the glaring rays of the sun as they bounced off the blue water of the bay and the ice and snow packs that accented the rest of northland's landscape. His weathered face was cut deep with wrinkles and blotched with leather brown and sunburn red; his scruffy whiskers were gray and unshaven. I couldn't explain it, but I sensed a down-to-earth nobility in this man that I immediately trusted. Spence seemed like a man of his word, and I felt that under his rough exterior he had a heart of gold. As far as I was concerned, he was the right man for the job.

Spence knew how to drive a hard bargain. He told Vern, "You buy the gas and the food. Then give me fifty dollars a day for eight days. If it takes longer makes no difference. If we get lucky and take less time, that not make difference either. I still get four hundred dollars worth of pay." With the price of gas and grub, those two hundred miles would cost over five hundred dollars. But Vern really had no alternative. He was in a weak bargaining position and both he and Spence knew it.

"Last time on this part of the bay for short hunting trip, weather kept us gone for many weeks," continued old Jimmy Spence, "and we eat plenty of goose because we had no more food." He added, "Finding drinkable water another big problem this time of year."

After closing the deal with Spence, Vern and I went to find Issaluk and settled up with him. Much to his pleasure, he would be flown back to Chesterfield Inlet and soon reunited with his family. Now a new question began to concern me...what would I do for a partner after Jimmy Spence got me off the bay? Spence and I would be landing at York Factory, which had been a bustling settlement during the peak of the fur trading days of the 1800s. Now, York Factory was no more than an abandoned site of old buildings and historic relics of a bygone era. After Vern and I talked it over, we decided that while he and the Canadian government recruited another Eskimo to complete the trip with me, I should keep traveling, probably relying on Cree guides, since we were now out of Eskimo territory. When Vern located another Eskimo travel companion, he would have him flown to wherever I was at that time. The plan suited me fine because I wanted to keep moving!

My two days of relaxation before hitting the trail ended up being hectic. I scoured the city for ten-gallon gasoline drums for our long haul, cleaned up and repaired our gear, and replenished supplies to meet the needs of traveling to York Factory and starting the trek up the Hayes River. As I canvassed Churchill in search of supplies, I stumbled into some rather interesting places. One was a small, run-down old mission, which held the first Lutheran Church service in North America. Its dark interior was still very beautiful, and just sitting there for a moment in the reverent atmosphere of the sanctuary was a big spiritual lift for me. It's strange, I thought to myself, that when we have to go to church we sometimes grow tired of it, but when we are without it we come to miss it very much.

The next morning Vern and I paid our second visit to Jerry Allan, head of Indian Affairs, whose help we'd enlisted in finding a companion to travel with me through the Hayes River country. He didn't have the good news we'd expected. "I'm sorry fellows, there isn't an Indian in Churchill that wants your job—not even for twenty dollars a day," he told us. "Plus," he added, "I'm not certain how you'd get them to York Factory." His later comment prompted us to make our way out to the Churchill airstrip to talk with Lamb Air. "Ya, it'd be possible to fly someone and some supplies into the Hayes area, say around the Fox River or Knee Lake, but we've lost two planes already this season and just plain don't have any available planes. Sorry," he said. This hadn't been a good day. Two strikes in a row: no guide, and no way to get him to the Hayes River if we found one. Vern and I went back to the Churchill Hotel for a lukewarm cup of the mud they called coffee and pondered our next strategies.

We hadn't had much luck depending on someone else to hire a guide; we decided our only option was to do our own recruitment. We literally hit every bar, building, and business in Churchill. Eventually, our efforts led us to Wilfred Fortin. Wilfred, like Jimmy Spence, was a Metis, or half breed. He guided part-time and worked for one of the businesses in Churchill. Educated by his parents, he'd spent his entire life on the rivers of the northern wilderness, being forced to cross rapids both upstream and downstream every time he journeyed into town. Fortin agreed to join me at York Factory and to travel upstream with me as far as Oxford House, located just north of Lake Winnipeg. We still faced the problem of how to get him there. With Wilfred's help, that problem was soon resolved. He convinced his employer, who owned the local petroleum business, to let his personal pilot fly him, Vern, and additional supplies to York Factory. It was agreed they would fly to the abandoned settlement two days after we'd left by canoe, following the coast so they could check on our progress. Our problems seemed solved if the weather would just cooperate.

The next morning Vern and I met Jimmy. "I'm taking my boy so I got someone to travel back with," he said, pointing to forty-seven year old Frank Spence. Frank was a quiet man, but I'd been told he could hold his own with the devil when he'd been drinking. I'd also been told he was as strong as an ox—"Once carried seven hundred pounds of flour on his back," someone had said. Even with Jimmy's years of experience and Frank's strength on our side, we waited on the piers by the big grain elevator until after ten o'clock waiting for the crashing waves to mellow.

"Young lad, you know how to properly tie a canoe for pullin'?" asked Jimmy, eyeing me.

"Not really," I replied.

"Then watch," he ordered with a stern yet friendly tone.

He tied the line in such a fashion that the bow of *Little Eric* sat in a cradle or Y-shaped piece of rope, tied securely to the thwart behind the front seat on each side. "That'll hold the bow up proper," Spence said, and with that we got into his freighter canoe and headed out of the harbor. This would be the last time *Little Eric* was towed. Soon we would be in river country where the canoe would finally be in the element it was created to handle—I hoped!

Not far from the mouth of the Churchill River, we saw the rolling backs of two to three dozen beluga or white whales, sometimes getting within a few yards of them. As we watched the whales pass, Frank offered, "We used to take people out to harpoon the whales, but now they say they've got mercury poisoning; ain't even good for the dogs to eat."

Mercury poison, I thought, *way up here—how unfortunate.*

An hour beyond Churchill, we spotted a large polar bear standing on the smooth rock of a peninsula marking Churchill Cape. With a locomotive-like snort, the fat bear plunged off the rock and into the cold water. I urged Spence in close enough to get some pictures, but he did so with more caution than Issaluk or Kukliak had ever shown. "Young lad," said Jim, "last time I was on this stretch of coast, one of them blasted bears came into our tent and ripped the arm off one of my friends before I could kill it—now I always sleep with a loaded gun by my side; I'd as soon as kill one of them bears as look at him."

"You sleep with your gun?" I exclaimed.

"You should start making it a practice," he replied, and from that night on I did. I recalled from my pre-trip reading that the stretch of coast around Churchill has the world's highest concentration of polar bears.

Once we had rounded the northern most point of the cape, I saw something I had not seen for what seemed like forever—long golden beaches of sand. As evening approached, the beaches appeared to glow brightly as a hundred thin lines of light shot out from the setting sun and poured onto the beaches through two small holes in the clouds. Were I not wearing a parka, it would have seemed like a summer evening on a lake back home in Minnesota.

We put into shore on a deserted sand bar south of Broad River and tried to have some tea and banic, a dense unleavened bread. However, the mosquitoes were fierce; face netting was necessary and to remove your glove for anything was an invitation never turned down by a bloodthirsty host of mosquitoes. The mosquitoes literally clouded around your face in such vast numbers that they darkened what remained of the dimming daylight. With our bodies completely covered to protect ourselves from the surroundings swarms, we talked—sitting there holding our tea as it was too difficult to remove one's face netting and take a sip without suffering numerous uncomfortable bites. The conversation soon turned serious as Jimmy told me of his life as an alcoholic. "Oh, I was a bad one, I was," he explained. "Sometimes I used to even drink rubbin' alcohol or shoe polish because I couldn't afford no liquor." On a very sincere note, he continued, "Near twenty years ago, I come home one night and my wife was nagging at me good for bein' drunk, and I slapped her one, but I was sober enough to know what I'd done, and I felt real bad. She wouldn't talk to me no more and I felt so bad," he repeated, "so I promised her I'd quit drinkin' and ain't had a drop since. For many years after that happened, I used to go sit in the bar, and resisting a drink hurt bad," he continued, "but I wouldn't drink none cause I knew what I'd done to my wife. I finally quit goin', been dry now for twenty years."

My admiration for the man grew enormously. Changing the subject, Jimmy asked, "What you got for snares?"

"I've got a couple," I offered.

"That ain't anywhere near enough," he shook his head. "We'll see if we can find some wire at York Factory. You'll need to rely on small game like rabbit when travelin' through the river country—especially with warmer weather comin'."

Jimmy made me feel my inexperience and lack of preparation for such travels, but as he tutored me for hours each day, I felt like the old fellow had adopted me as his understudy. He never put me down, and in his own rough way, his chiding about my inexperience was comforting. I could tell he cared, and I sought to absorb what he had to offer like a sponge soaks up water.

Even with good weather, we had to travel slowly across Nelson's Shoal, as it could quickly transition from deep water to shallow rock ledges and submerged boulders. Thirty minutes north of Nelson River and miles from shore, we struck a rock in one of the shallows, cracking part of the planking in the bow of Jimmy's canoe and causing slow but continuous leakage. Nelson's Shoal covers a wide area, and because our progress was slow, we had not made it across the shoal before the tide moved out. We were grounded on the rocky mire over five miles from both the shore and the water's edge. This was the type of situation that had taken the life of more than one inexperienced canoeist. With about an eight-hour wait before the tide would return, I found myself tempted to wander away from the canoes, just exploring the small pools of water trapped among the rocks. But walking over slippery rocks in a tidal flat of soft mud I found my legs wouldn't carry me very far or very fast, and Jimmy warned that the area was so shallow that an incoming tide backed by a wind could swiftly sweep across the mire like a tidal wave. We took no chances. We tied *Little Eric* and Jimmy's canoe together, and we stayed within a few feet of their safety as we waited for the tide.

After some banic caked with peanut butter and jam, the three of us sat in a half-awake state, with one ear alertly listening for the gurgle of returning water. The hum, which soon rang in our ears, however, was not that of running water, but that of a small airplane engine—no doubt Vern and Wilfred Fortin on their way to York Factory. Combing the sky with our eyes, we spotted the dark body of the plane far out toward the open water. I quickly dug out the two emergency blankets that we carried for emergency signals. If both bright yellow blankets were out, we needed help, if only one was out, everything was fine. Having no trouble other than tides and weather, I laid out one blanket. It was a useless signal, for they were eagerly searching the water's edge for us. They were not looking nearly five miles inland where our two canoes were tethered together. The plane soon left without any idea of our whereabouts. Vern, I figured, would be afraid we had drowned. With the plane gone, we resumed our patient wait for the tide until around mid-evening. We heard the lapping of waves approaching in the distance and watched as the tide came in swirling and burying the coast in its cold depths. We had one unanticipated surprise. The tide did not come in alone, it brought a thick layer of heavy fog with it, and the veil of fog got thicker as the water got deeper. We had to wait for water deep enough to float our heavy load so we could inch toward shore, but before the water was deep enough to move, a northeast wind started to rock the sea now totally enveloped in a dense white fog. The three of us used paddles to pole the canoes through the shallow water, not being able to see over twenty feet ahead of us. We were like blind men as we worked slowly closer to the shore, moved more by the foaming waves then our own power.

Little Eric towed well, but it needed steady forward progress to pull straight and combat the effects of the wind hitting its high bow and stern. In these conditions, our forward progress was too slow and the wind toyed at will with *Little Eric*. I watched horrified as the wind tipped our river transportation on its side and then filled it with water, the first wave leading the way for others. *Little Eric* was swamped! There seemed little hope of saving it and still keeping ourselves afloat, but before cutting it loose we made one desperate attempt to save it.

We pulled *Little Eric* along side Jim's canoe and with my knife I cut free the supplies we had lashed into it. I reached into the icy water up to my armpits to gather the supplies and tossed them into Jim's canoe. As I worked my fingers instinctively wrapped around the gunwale of *Little Eric* for support; with the next wave *Little Eric* rose slightly and then bashed into Jim's canoe with hammer like force. I jerked my hand back and cringed in pain. Again and again *Little Eric* pounded at us until Jim started to cut its towline to save us and his canoe from going down. At the last moment he stuffed a pack between the two canoes and Frank did the same at the bow. With little feeling in my flattened fingers, Frank and I bailed with fury. Then, with a feat of strength that made me believe perhaps he had carried seven hundred pounds of flour as people said, Frank hollered at me to grab hold of *Little Eric*. With flexing muscles of arm and back, we hoisted *Little Eric* across the gunwale of Jim's canoe, carefully slipping it back into the bay on the other side, waterless and floating. With our movement still paralyzed by fog and shallow water and guided by the wind alone, we didn't dare try to tow the canoe again. Three lifejackets were dropped over the side of Jim's canoe and we lashed *Little Eric* alongside, but each time a wave splashed between the two tightly tied canoes, a spurt of water shot out from between them like a geyser, showering our canoe with icy saltwater spray.

It seemed to take an eternity, but we finally worked our way to a mud flat and the edge of the fog. The two hundred yards between the shore and us was covered in thick gooey mud that squished into everything, as we got ready to beach our canoes. Once on shore, we acted quickly to make a fire, set up our tents, and drink some warm tea. All other chores would wait until morning.

The next day we managed to travel only three hours before a northeast wind came to life, forcing us to beach at the mouth of the Nelson River within sight of the unfinished bridge started there before York Factory and Port Nelson were abandoned to establish the shipping port at Churchill. One reason they moved the port to Churchill still lay trapped in the shallow Nelson River. It was the rusting skeleton of a small ship. Looking upstream toward the dark outline of the unfinished pier, Jim pointed out remains of two other ships, which had been lost in this unreliable harbor. Our landing was much less eventful than those of the half-sunken ships; we landed on a sandy beach that appeared to be the nesting ground for several thousand mosquitoes and black flies all obviously in need of a meal. Once again we were forced to wear our head netting for sanity. It also seemed to help deter these mini-beasts of prey if one made frequent trips through the smoke—permeating one's clothes with the permanent odor of smoke. Even the large hordes of dragonflies buzzing about seemed to make little dent in the mosquito population. In Minnesota we sometimes joke that the mosquito is the state bird. Even with that background for context, this was by far the worst I'd ever seen. Were you not totally covered, I suspect insanity would have overtaken one quickly.

To reach York Factory we had to round Marsh Point, a crossing that would depend solely on the weather. This was another stretch that was very shallow far out into the bay. Strong winds could swiftly turn that entire point into a bad nightmare. The winds never seemed to die down, and every time they did, it seemed the tide was out and we could not travel. We sat for days only miles from our final destination on Hudson Bay.

Anxious to be off Hudson Bay and into river country, I paced up and down the shore, and to my great surprise, I found some nine-inch spikes and four old cannon balls, three still nearly round and one rather flattened. Caked with tidal mud and pitted and corroded by saltwater, these artifacts had likely been carried from the fort that once stood at York Factory. It was hard to imagine the story that went with these relics, but being treasures worth keeping, I tucked them away in the canoe. Vern would probably want them for his museum collection.

At eight o'clock p.m. on July 17, we finally escaped from shore and maneuvered our canoes across the whale-populated mouth of the Nelson River. The sea was rolling gently as we approached Marsh Point, which had been given its name for a good reason. It was a low area, nearly level with the sea. It was indeed marshy—not forested with willow, balsam, and spruce as the rest of the shoreline. As we rounded Marsh Point, I turned and cast my last look at the bay. It was calmly rolling now, painted by a setting orange sun. I wasn't sure if I was telling a friend or an enemy goodbye. My look took in not only what I could see, but in my mind I went back over the 1,400 miles I'd crossed and the host of encounters, good and bad, that I'd had on that massive body of water. By God's grace and with good companions, I'd made it this far. Now I turned to face the Hayes River!

Jimmy Spence guides Barry across the Hudson Bay.

Vern and Jimmy Spence at York Factory.

Into the Wilderness

"Therefore I tell you, do not worry about your life, what you will eat or drink; or about your body, what you will wear. Is not life more important than food, and the body more important than clothes?" (Matthew 6:25)

Journal Excerpt: July 22, 1970

"Put in a grueling fourteen hour day and crossed fifteen rapids—some of which should have been called falls as they dropped at least five feet in a short distance."

Vern was most relieved to see us! "You're days late, and Vern's ready to have a heart attack," said Wilfred Fortin, my new partner to be. "When he couldn't spot you from the plane, he was sure you'd drowned. He's been so worried, I'm even glad to see you!"

As I looked at the rest of the gathering on shore, I began to wonder who had told me the village of York Factory was deserted. Old Jim was watching the people collect on the bank and I heard him ask Wilfred Fortin quietly, "Is the game manager here?" With a *no* reply, Jim and Frank breathed a little easier about the geese lying in our canoes.

"I thought this place was abandoned," I said. "There must be more people here now than there has been for decades." A group of about twenty students and a couple of advisors from the University of Manitoba were living at the village for the summer. They were staying in a small gray house they had already restored. The students were there to map out the entire settlement and to make blueprints of the buildings, especially the old York House. "That building is something!" said Vern. "We'll have to get some pictures of you, *Little Eric,* and Spence in front of it."

"Bosh, not me," grumbled Jim.

"We've got to," Vern said excitedly. "I found where you scratched your name into the wall forty years ago."

By the time we'd had a meal spiced with conversation of our trip from Churchill and the restoration taking place at York Factory, it was time to sleep. I still didn't know much about my companion to be, Wilfred Fortin. Wilfred was shorter and of smaller frame than me. He probably weighed less than 150 pounds. His jet-black hair, edged with gray, was cut short and always hid under a baseball cap. He sported a thin black mustache barely evident against his dark complexion. Vern shared with me that Wilfred had been plenty drunk by the time they flew into York Factory. Other than his bent to overindulge in drink, he seemed like a lighthearted and hardworking guy. Perhaps that was a good combination for the miles ahead. I was relieved to know, however, that there were no liquor stores in the hundreds of wilderness miles we were about to face.

First thing next morning, Vern, Jim, Frank Spence, and I went to explore the York House. It was a mammoth three-story building with peeling white paint and faded red shingles. In years long past, this building had served as the Hudson Bay Trading Post and as the primary storage facility for furs and supplies for much of the North Country. It was a maze of huge open rooms. In many ways, the building resembled the hull of an old sailing ship. "It wasn't carpenters but shipbuilders who made this place," I observed. Huge tree roots perhaps a foot thick in the middle were used as angle supports along the roof and wall, some helping to support thirty-foot hewn timbers up to sixteen inches in diameter. Protruding above the third story was a small tower in the shape of a hexagon that was once used to watch for incoming ships. From up there I could see the rest of the village, largely covered by brush and trees after decades of abandonment. Several tumbled down shacks, which once served as homes, now rested dangerously near the sixty-foot banks, which the river continually wore away. Far to the south end of the village, I could see the weathered brown roof of an empty steeple. I was told the church bell that had once been there now hung in the mission I had visited at Churchill.

Vern led us downstairs to one of the storage rooms where scratched on the wall were the words: "Jim Spence, July 16, 1930." I scratched my name on the wall underneath it: "Barry Lane, July 18, 1970." Despite Jim's grumbling, which I had a hard time accepting as sincere, we posed for Vern's pictures next to our inscriptions.

Wilfred and I were more anxious to be done with the pictures than the others, for we wanted to be well on our way upstream before the tide went out; its strong pull at the mouth of the Hayes could possibly prevent our departure. For this leg of our journey, we mounted a four-horsepower outboard to the side of *Little Eric*'s stern. We estimated that the outboard would push us up to eight miles-per-hour south while the Hayes often ran at ten miles-per-hour north, leaving a two mile-per-hour difference for the bow man to make up with arm strength and paddle. To portage the outboard and ten-gallon drums of gasoline wasn't going to be easy; however, making progress going upstream would be nearly impossible for two men without assistance from the four-horsepower kicker.

As we were about to push out into the river, Jim Spence

came up to me one last time. Reaching into his pocket, the old fellow handed me half a dozen rabbit snares. "Here," he said, "this is all the good wire I could find. Take them. You might need them." Then, hesitating, he added, "Young lad, take care."

Looking up river, Wilfred stated, "It'd be best to follow the steep bank; water will be deeper there." Jim, Frank, and Vern followed us for a distance in Spence's canoe taking pictures of our launch into the wilderness. Once they turned back, Wilfred and I were not likely to see any other humans for weeks.

I had been waiting to embrace the rugged beauty of the Hayes River area. We were following the same route traversed nearly three hundred years earlier by the fur traders and their heavy York boats and freighter canoes. We were going through the heartland of a wilderness that even now was virtually unchanged and uninhabited by man. The brown river appeared deceptively calm for it was characterized by a stiff northbound current. On the west bank of the river was a one-hundred-foot cliff of eroded sand spotted with patches of light green grasses and clumps of purple, yellow, and white wildflowers. The top of the bank was forested with spruce trees standing so close together it appeared to be impossible to walk between them. The opposite bank was consistently lower, covered with long grasses, and a forest that came to the river's edge. It was a land of true natural beauty, and I loved it. But as I looked around, I seldom saw a place level enough for a sleeping bag, let alone a tent. Finding a place to camp wasn't going to be easy.

Once beyond the reach of the tide, Wilfred and I stopped on an island in the middle of the half-mile-wide river where we ate lunch and planned our route using strip maps I'd cut from detailed topographical maps before leaving. I'd cut them in a three-inch strip to reduce unnecessary weight. Much to my surprise and pleasure, we ate in real comfort—the swarm of mosquitoes, which had continually attacked the last few days on Hudson Bay and at York Factory, seemed to have stayed on the coast.

We quickly learned that we needed to stop every two hours or so to switch positions; the stern man's arm and hand went numb holding the vibrating outboard in place, and the bow man tired from exhaustive paddling.

I had been anxious to see how *Little Eric* would handle on the river after encountering nothing but trouble with it on Hudson Bay. "Vern told me if we both looked over the same side it would tip," said Wilfred. "I was starting to wonder what I'd gotten myself into." But with a heavy load of gas and supplies lying low in the center of the canoe, we found this one of the most stable river canoes either of us had been in. Between engine and paddle, we soon learned to maneuver with ease and accuracy in the strong current.

Someone had told me the only reason the original birch bark canoes had a high bow and stern was to keep powder horns dry for the old muzzle loaded-type guns they used. Although Wilfred and I had no powder horn, we traveled as the early voyageurs did with a gun propped against the bow. For supplies we carried only essentials: flour, rolled oats, tea, some dried meat, and salt. This meant our lifeline was the land. It was the bowman's responsibility to both paddle and hunt for the day's food supply. Now out of the natural refrigeration of the far north, we'd have to rely on smaller game.

The last day Spence and I had spent on the bay I was still wearing my snowmobile suit and parka despite clear and sunny skies. Only one day off the bay and I stripped off everything and frolicked in the river like a child in a sprinkler. It was a bit cold, but it felt great just to bathe. I used my hunting knife to scrape my teeth clean and worked for fifteen minutes to wash all the Hudson Bay salt spray out of my hair. My mustache whiskers were getting so long I used my lower teeth to pull them into my mouth and nibbled off the ends.

Mornings on the Hayes were different than they had been on the bay. No longer were hours spent lingering over a cup of tea as we waited to see what the weather would do. Now, once Wilfred and I gulped down some rolled oats and tea, we paused only long enough to scour our brown stained teacups with sand and pack up. Then we'd renew our battle with the Hayes River, slowly inching south. The rapid current would swirl past our little kicker causing it to momentarily pull sideways and hum with a bogged down pitch. We regularly put in twelve- to six-teen-hour days.

Our southward progress was at all times an uphill battle and we plugged along slowly against the current. Once beyond the fork where God's River and the Hayes met, our progress became even harder due to the narrowing of the Hayes River. Now the current was relentlessly strong. In its swift current it was not uncommon to stay parallel with the same shoreline bush for several minutes as we struggled with both paddle and kicker to move forward. The banks of light brown sand crowned with waxy willows, light green poplar trees, dark spruce, and patches of foot-high swamp grass painted the rugged land with a beauty that made one stop and thank God for His handiwork. Some-times I just wished the scenery would pass by a little faster. In some areas, we managed to progress only one or two miles in an hour's time.

Day after day we heard no human or mechanical sounds other than those we made ourselves; our company was the call of birds and the gurgle of the river rushing over the rocks. At night the snaps of a dying fire, the haunting call of a loon, and the cry of a distant wolf became the everyday sounds of our journey.

While good campsites were difficult to find, some were

truly a gift from God. On one occasion when we were particularly hot and tired after hours of travel and a burning sun, Wilfred spotted a natural spring on shore. The water was so cold we were forced to drink slowly so our teeth wouldn't ache! The area also boasted an unending patch of ripe red strawberries, an adequate supply of driftwood for our fire, and a flat area to pitch our tent.

Some days were tougher than others. One day when the sun was blazing down on my arms and neck, noon came and went with no food. By evening I was suffering from cherry-colored sunburn and a hammering headache. "Don't you wish you had a tan like me?" joked Wilfred. We intended to stop early, but reached our decision about an hour too late, for by evening we had left behind the sandy river banks we'd been traveling past; forested banks now extended to the water's edge on both sides of the river. We landed three times but couldn't find an area big enough for the tent, and finally, as darkness enfolded us, we put into shore and erected the tent at a forty-five-degree angle facing the river.

"Dirty devil," said Wilfred. "What a way to sleep." It was almost like trying to sleep standing up, and as I rolled out our sleeping bags they looked like toboggans ready to shoot down a steep hill. My throbbing head felt like it was swelling and shrinking with each beat of my heart. Fortunately, I didn't feel much like eating. I settled for three aspirins and a cup of river water. "This is the first medication I've had to take on this trip," I told Wilfred.

"Well, dirty devil! Let's hope it's the last," he replied. Picking up his tea and a piece of dried meat Wilfred reflected, "Looks like tomorrow we shoot anything we can."

With my senses rather deadened by pain, I wasn't doing a lot of deep thinking, but a scripture verse came to mind, *"Take no thought for what you will eat, the Lord knows you have those needs and will provide ... "* then I couldn't help but think how much I hoped that was true for us. I was so tired; the moss we had thrown under the tent to help level it made a soft bed, and despite our uncomfortable position, it appeared we would both get the rest we needed. Tomorrow we would worry about food.

The next morning we woke to the quiet babble of geese. Wilfred carefully opened the tent flap to see three geese sitting on the shore just a few yards in front of our tent. He carefully looked down the crooked sights and bent barrel of the .22 we carried. We'd jokingly named the gun Opportunity, for that rifle was our biggest opportunity to keep eating. Wilfred's aim and God's grace prevailed. We would have goose to eat!

On July 21, we met our first rapids on the Hayes, but they were short enough to power up with an open throttle, if the bowman paddled like crazy. Going upstream in rapids was a lot different than going with the rapids downstream! For one thing, progress was slow. The current was always trying to grab at the canoe and turn it sideways. Other than avoiding rocks, the hardest part of going upstream was keeping the canoe parallel to the current.

I appreciated Wilfred's knowledge of upstream canoeing and his willingness to teach me. When we came to rapids we couldn't canoe up, Wilfred would search the entire river ahead before announcing, "Dirty devil, we can't run that one," and then with a quick second check he'd say, "that's the best place to land over there." He looked not only for a safe, suitable place to land as far upstream as possible, but also went to the quieter side of the river. You had to quickly assess the shoreline, and if it appeared you might have to portage part of the rapids, you had to consider which side offered the shortest portage and best place to re-enter the river. After years of experience, Wilfred was an expert at reading rivers.

Sometimes we could not motor and paddle up a rapids. Our next option was to get in the water and walk the canoe up. We'd wade into the river hanging onto *Little Eric's* gunwale, Wilfred at the bow, and I at the stern. "Always stay on the shore side of the canoe," warned Wilfred. "Try to stay away from getting on the outside of the canoe by the rapids." I listened. We'd inch forward clinging to *Little Eric* with one hand, and to the shoreline vegetation and rocks with the other. "When you grab brush always grab a handful," said Wilfred, "and make sure its green, not dead, before you depend on it for a good anchor." Footing wasn't the best in the swift, rocky water, so a hand-hold was an essential thing, especially when standing in rushing water nearly up to one's armpits. The current was continually trying to pull the bow out into midstream, putting stress on Wilfred to hold it in. At my end the current was always force-fully pushing in, putting stress on me to hold it straight with the current, for only then could we pull our way along the shore with any degree of success. Maneuvering around rocks required even greater teamwork. But the hard wet work of walking with the canoe up a rapid was worth it, for we were not forced to unload our supplies and pack them across on our backs through an area where there were no established portages.

Even though we were exhausted by evening, the work wasn't over when we landed for the night. We still needed to set up camp, secure the canoe and our packs, collect firewood, and fix something to eat. If we made camp early enough, we'd often rig a pole or two for fishing and put out our rabbit snares in the surrounding woods. On one particular occasion we were camped at the foot of a large rapid we would need to traverse first thing the next morning. Listening to the roar of the nearby water, I lay awake for a while thinking of all the things I'd been through, and that night I prayed, like I tried to do every night, but didn't always manage. *"Lord, you've been with me a mighty long time on this trip, and if you'll just help us get to Lake Winnipeg, I think we'll make it—and Lord, please let my loved ones know I'm all right. They've got enough on their minds without worrying about me. Amen. Oh yes, and Lord, Wilfred and I could sure use some food tomorrow."*

Early the next morning, we were forced to get into the water to walk the canoe through the biggest rapids we'd yet encountered. I promptly started things off on the wrong foot—literally—taking only two steps before going into deep swift water. Wilfred just kept laughing and saying, "That was a mighty deep hole!" I was quite literally wet from the neck down for the next sixteen hours. We crossed fifteen rapids, some of which might properly have been called waterfalls, as they dropped over five feet in two or three closely related step formations.

Now in the very heart of whitewater country, Wilfred and I could no longer paddle up the river, nor could we walk the canoe up the rapids as we had done with some of the first rough water we'd encountered. I became Wilfred's pupil at a new skill. We found it necessary to pole the canoe upstream. It was almost like walking the canoe upstream without stepping into the swift water. Carefully we would reach forward, firmly anchor the paddle among the rocks, and then with a tightened grip around the paddle we would pull forward another foot. Poling is a skill and a team effort, making it necessary for one man to hold the canoe still while the other picked a new, firm position, which he could hold while his partner released his prying point and sought another. Wilfred prepared me in the event we'd lose our hold and *Little Eric* would become a runaway craft with only the following bit of knowledge, "We can't take time to turn the canoe around in that water," he said, "and if it turns sideways, we'll surely lose it, so if we start downstream we'll have to run the rapids backwards." He explained, "It's the same as

shooting one front ways, you just can't see where you're going."
Comforting!

I didn't have to learn to steer backwards, because most of
the rapids could not be approached by poling, as they were too
swift and steep. So we turned to the next best thing, a line. That
was one thing that amazed me about Wilfred—his ability to
judge the best and easiest way to cross a rapid. When I mentioned his skill he said, "Well, dirty devil! I ain't gonna carry all
this gear and that overgrown canoe until I have to!" Tying one
of the knots like old Spence had taught me around the brace
in the bow; Wilfred ran the rope to the open streamside of the
canoe, so that when pulled from shore the rope lay above the
waterline and diagonally across the entire bow.

"When you're on shore," warned Wilfred, "make sure you've
got good footing, 'cause the man in the water—namely me—is
going to be depending on you. It's too noisy to yell," he continued, "so when I shake my head yes, pull like the devil, and if I
shake my head no, then slowly slacken the rope. If I hold up a
fist, hold the rope where it is."

It became evident that lining was merely an extension of
what we'd done while walking the canoe. From shore it was
my job not only to hold the bow in from the outward pushing
current, but on Wilfred's nod to also pull it forward, and at all
times have a firm hold on the canoe, so if he slipped he could
grab the canoe for support.

To accomplish this, I had to station myself behind a rock
or tree for my own support. The rope had to be at a forty-
five-degree angle to the bow so my pull was both inward and
forward. Wilfred was in the water with the stern of the canoe
trying to hold it straight against the force fighting to push it in,
but unlike before, the water he now stood in tumbled with a
deafening rumble, and threatened with a swirling, boiling surface intent on stealing his footing.

Trying to anticipate everything we did a step ahead of doing it, we moved into proper position with care. Then with Wilfred signaling me from his insecure position in the water, I started to pull hand over hand feeling like I was competing in a tug of war. I let the excess rope drop at my feet. My eyes were on *Little Eric* and Wilfred who struggled along with the canoe, both of his hands clenched tightly over the gunwale. When pulled to the safety of my position, Wilfred anchored one arm on shore and supported *Little Eric,* while I ranged ahead for new footing, moving us twenty feet upstream each time we accomplished it. Our first lining attempt was a success!

One of the most common methods of getting the canoe around a rapid involved a combination of lining and rolling. Often we would line up as far as the base of a falls, and there we would find the water too deep, too swift, and the angle too steep to take on with a line. Frequently these falls were bordered by large outcroppings of the Canadian Shield resembling a weatherworn sidewalk of rock. If the terrain was level enough, we could roll *Little Eric* across the granite as if on wheels, again saving us the unloading of our supplies. Wilfred and I cut down and peeled a three-inch poplar tree and cut it into two-yard-long pieces, a process that took about twenty minutes. We placed our log rollers about six feet apart, then with one of us pushing from each side of the canoe, we would roll *Little Eric* forward; continually moving the back roller forward as the canoe passed over it. It was a bit like the peeled poles were playing leapfrog.

Our attempt to make our way up a particularly challenging rapid nearly ended in disaster. The rapid was situated in a deep ravine; at one point it dropped nearly ten feet like a mini Niagara Falls. We thought we could line up the west side and agreed to give it a try. Wilfred would be in the water at the stern and I would be the lineman on shore. We managed to get *Little Eric* halfway through. I was struggling to prevent the plunging water from pulling the bow away, but the decision to stop would have to come from Wilfred, as I couldn't loosen the rope when he depended on it being taut for support. I stood, anchored behind a rock, with my arms painfully stretched out, holding the canoe in position. Wilfred was in trouble too. He could no longer swing the stern into the current, and at last motioned for me to come back. I fed out the slack in the rope, and he worked the canoe toward shore. I started to work my way toward the canoe but as I stepped around a tree near shore, my feet slipped out from under me on the wet rock. I fell into the heart of the rapid and found myself racing helplessly downstream and body surfing over the ten-foot waterfall! I clung instinctively to the rope. I smacked violently into the bottom of the canoe at least six feet behind the bow. Wilfred saw what happened and reached for something to hold onto, but his hand landed only on a flat rock, his fingertips dragging uselessly across it as the canoe started to move downstream with me still trapped underneath it. Wilfred's hand finally found an outcropping he could cling to, and as he pulled the canoe into shallow water, I emerged from under the canoe and managed to gain an insecure hold on slippery rock. From this disabled position, we worked the canoe to shore an inch at a time, resigned to the fact that we'd better portage this one, and grateful that we still could.

We searched the banks and found an old trail. With a small folding camp saw and hatchet, we went to work like a couple of beavers brushing out the trail, removing a few scrawny trees and cutting protruding limbs from many more. It took a half-hour before we were ready to return for our supplies. Since it was a short portage, we made two trips each rather than trying to pack everything across in one load. The canoe, even when empty, was very heavy to lift up the three-foot rock wall to our portage trail, but that was the best landing spot nature had provided. Using our two log rollers, we managed to lift the canoe up to the portage trail. The path was level enough for both of us to carry the canoe rather than burdening one man with its 160-pound bulk.

Sometimes moving upstream needed to give way to securing the day's food supply. Stopping at the base of a falls, which offered an unusually flat rock surface to roll the canoe across, we caught a couple of frogs, and with a straight hook and line tied snuggly to the end of a willow pole, went fishing. With the end of my pole soon arched into the water, I staggered backward to shallow water dragging with me a nice northern pike. We soon added a couple more small fish to our catch. Our stringer wasn't impressive, but it added up to another meal.

One doesn't carry a lot of extra supplies into the wilderness, and the rough conditions can take its toll on equipment. By now some of our outboard's wiring had been replaced with anything that would conduct an electrical current, and a bent nail had replaced the cotter key. In the middle of poling up a rapids Wilfred lost his paddle. "I wonder if my paddle will ever reach York Factory," Wilfred pondered. We made our way to shore and found a large fallen spruce tree. Using my paddle as a model, Wilfred hewed a new paddle from the trunk of the tree over the course of the next two hours. The blade was slightly narrower than desired, and it was heavier—but it was fully functional.

Wilfred and I took turns cooking. One evening he brewed up another thick soup composed mainly of flour, river water, and whatever we had to put in it for meat—usually fish. While he cooked, I covered a flat area of rock with moss and set our tent on the prepared area. We felt like we were living luxurious lives when we could sleep on a cushioned surface. As we sat next to the drying warmth of the campfire while our bodies slowly thawed from the inside out with the warm tea, I counted seventy-four small red welts with a white dot in the middle on just my left arm. "Man that stuff itches!" I told Wilfred. "Are you sure that isn't poison ivy?"

Looking at the blotches in the firelight, Wilfred said, "Ya, I'm sure—but it's a nice collection of black fly bites."

"Thanks," I responded, "but it's a collection I'd just as soon do without." The mosquitoes weren't bothering us, but for the past two days the black flies had been unbearable.

By now I'd lost count of the number of rapids we'd conquered. Our maps, although accurate to four miles to the inch, were not detailed enough to show every rapids or island. I believe the map indicated we'd eventually cross around 120 rapids—but in reality, we'd likely see more white water than the map actually showed. The same was true for the maze of islands we encountered; where the map showed there were four, we would find dozens, and it was generally a blind guess which route would offer the least resistance in our uphill battle. I'm sure some of our detours around various islands resulted in more lining or walking of the canoe than was necessary had we chosen a different route. "Remember that advertisement of Mr. Schield that said, 'From the Arctic to the Gulf of Mexico and walk less than ten miles on dry land?'" I questioned Wilfred.

"Ya, I remember," he said wearily. "He forgot to say anything about the fifty miles we'd walk in the water." We both smiled at the irony of our situation.

After weeks of travel, the land had been getting flatter and swampier and many of the rapids were less wicked than those we'd already left behind. Once back in languid water, we started to see waterfowl again, a welcome sight to hungry travelers. Looking at the limited amount of meat of the young fowl we'd recently shot for dinner, Wilfred said, "The first day we go hungry that old man starts paying me forty dollars a day rather than twenty."

"Relax," I tried to console him, "I left Vern with a list of supplies to fly into Knee Lake, including more gasoline and plenty of food staples. With luck we'll get there tomorrow."

Traveling against the Hayes River, more miles were spent going upstream than down.

Lining Little Eric upstream.

Conquering the Wilderness

"The Lord is my strength and my song; He has become my salvation ..." (Exodus 15:2)

Journal Excerpt: July 29, 1970

"We covered a one mile portage today between Max Lake and Logan Lake. Sweat was running into my eyes, flies were unmerciful, and the strain of the tump line across my forehead caused cramps in my neck muscles. I carried 160 pounds of supplies non-stop across the portage—a load comparable to what the voyageurs would have carried across this same portage a hundred years or more before me."

It was our third straight day of putting in a wet twelve to fourteen hours of travel. In addition to being in and out of the river water, it had been raining steadily. Shrouded in a light drizzle, we made our way up the last of more than seventy rapids in a forty-mile stretch just north of Knee Lake. The sun was starting to set, and our wet clothing clung to our bodies chilling us to the point where our teeth chattered. To avoid further chill we decided to put into shore to change into some dry clothes and make some tea.

We moved off the river and tied up in the underbrush. No sooner had we landed than a light plane flew overhead. "I bet that's the old man," said Wilfred. "I'll build a signal fire." As he tried to coax fire out of wet wood, I dug out our bright yellow signal blanket and quickly tossed it over our packs, but both our blanket and smoke were too slow in coming, and went unseen. "They must have just flown in the cache," I said. "We're almost to Knee Lake."

We talked it over as we downed our tea and decided to push on to Knee Lake. We reached the lake in the inky blackness of night. Not a hint of light in the sky except a few jagged flashes of lightning. The lake was alive with three-foot waves, and by the time we reached the shore of an island, it was raining so hard we wouldn't have been able to see had it been daylight.

The lightning flashes disclosed only a barricade of willows lining the shore. But drenched, cold, and blinded by night, that's where we landed. We unloaded our tent, personal gear, the food pack, and tied *Little Eric* securely to the shoreline with both a bow and stern line. Shouldering our packs, we headed inland where the hard rain only trickled through the dense growth of trees. We fumbled around in the darkness until finding an area big enough for the tent; there in the middle of a mossy swamp full of rotting trees we set up camp.

In wet misery we dug out the Coleman stove, which hadn't seen use since the bay, and tried to pump our systems full of warm tea and a couple of hot cups of rolled oats. We slipped out of our wet clothes and threw them outside the tent. There was no use in trying to dry them that night. Wilfred and I slipped into whatever combination of dry clothes we could find.

"Wilfred," I said.

"Ya," he replied.

"Welcome to Knee Lake."

His only reply was his favorite expression when things weren't going well, "Dirty devil."

Next morning we emerged from our rain-drenched tent into the tangled thicket of trees in which we had camped and from which a steady stream of water still dripped as if it were raining. Wilfred and I set out to comb the shores of Knee Lake in search of the red flag that was to mark the cache we desperately needed. Both our supply of gasoline and staples were nearly exhausted. We'd been re-boiling tea bags and had only a few cups of rolled oats and flour left. The lake was still rolling from the previous night's storm as we made our way along the east bank for six miles carefully watching the shoreline.

We found no cache. It was supposed to be left on the north end of the lake, so at that point we cut across, searching an island in the middle of the lake before continuing to the west shore. The island was beautiful and looked like a well-kept park, but offered no sign of the much-needed cache we were looking for. With the waves rocking Wilfred and me as if we were in a twenty-foot cradle, we reached the other side of the lake. We found long stretches of sand beaches ten to twelve feet wide surrounded by crystal-clear water shimmering with agates and other small colored stones, but no cache.

As we slipped silently along the beach, we scared up a flock of thirty geese, and our minds both registered the same thought: easy game, needed food. We landed well before reaching them and swiftly pulled *Little Eric* up on the sand. We dug out Opportunity and some shells, but the keen eyesight of the birds had detected us and they melted into the underbrush. Search as we would, Wilfred and I could only find a few stray feathers.

As we walked back to the canoe, we decided that the beach would make an excellent campsite and decided to move there once we found the cache. Then we discovered large bear tracks and changed our minds again in favor of the other side of the lake as a more suitable campsite.

We continued our search down the beach and backtracked up the river but found no cache. Then Wilfred said he thought he saw something just a bit farther downstream. "Would have been mighty easy for us the pass that cache on the river last night," he said. So we went back downstream to check out his sighting.

Sitting about fifty feet back from shore, we saw a canvas lashed between two trees. Closer investigation on foot disclosed the rough spruce frame of two huge tents, some rusted pots and pans, a ladder, and the eight-foot canvas Wilfred had seen from the river. "Must have been used by commercial fisherman at one time," said Wilfred. Then, as if to add proof to what he'd just said, we found an old rotting net approximately one hundred yards long, now containing only about ten yards of good netting. "It ain't much," said Wilfred, holding the mess of tangled threads in his hands, "but maybe we can get some netting out of it."

We took it with us and returned to camp, glad to have found the net but disgusted that we had not found the cache. Tossing our wet gear into *Little Eric,* we made our way back to one of the sandy beaches opposite the shore where we had seen the bear tracks.

Our equipment was a mess after the push up the Hayes. We set up the tent and brushed it clean with a spruce bough. I washed my clothes in a natural tub formed in a nearby rock; much like a washing machine, the water swirled in with every wave and then trickled out slowly through a dozen small cracks. I placed both sets of my clothes in the hole and while nature did the washing, I cleaned myself up in the lake. I was a little shocked when I returned to find all my clothes missing. Wearing everything I had—my hat and boots—I spent at least half an hour combing the shoreline for my clothes. I didn't find every-thing, but at least I knew I wouldn't have to resort to snaring rabbits to make a covering for myself! We scoured our black-ened pans with sand and strung lines to dry our clothes. Finally, we set about unraveling the now treasured net we'd found. If we could get some food by morning, we would push on toward the Cree settlement of Oxford House.

Despite the gaping holes in the net, Wilfred ran it between our island and a neighboring one. While he did, I made a pan of banic out of flour, baking powder, and lard. Our supplies were nearly gone. The net immediately proved worthwhile. For our evening meal we had four fish: a sucker, a walleye, a northern, and a whitefish. We fried them, using the last of our lard. Wilfred and I found a dead sucker washed up on shore by the waves, and with it for bait, we again put a hook and line on a willow pole. By darkness we had four more fish, and by morning our net had captured twelve more. We lacked lard or even animal fat for frying them; we would have to smoke them.

We moved into the shelter of the trees and built a wall of green brush over which we draped my poncho and the tarp used to cover our gear. Next we made a low table out of green willow poles, pounding a forked stick in each of the four corners and covering the frame with twenty more poles placed just inches apart. We built a strong hot fire of drift wood and added wet rotting birch wood from a nearby stump. It sent up a solid screen of smoke, which our brushed-in shelter retained rather well despite the wind. On top of our smoking table, we placed the fillets of fish. As Wilfred tended the fire, keeping it both burning and smoking, as well as turning the golden fillets, I took the entrails from all sixteen fish and melted them down over our campfire to collect grease. There isn't much fat on a fish, but we got enough grease to mix with the last of our baking powder and some flour for another pan of banic. It was a sickly yellow color but at least provided some bread for our meal.

It took until late in the afternoon, but the fillets Wilfred turned out were as good as those from any smokehouse. We now had meat, bread, and we could continue reusing our tea bags although the tea was getting so weak it hardly had any color or taste left. I was perturbed that Vern had never arrived with the cache we'd agreed he'd leave for us on Knee Lake, but at this point I was willing to concede that bad weather or some other barrier must have prevented him from being there. God was continually gracious, and once again we had what we needed to survive.

It was apparent that our plane wasn't coming, so we decided to leave at daybreak. With that settled, we roamed our little island with renewed zest. We found a huge patch of mushrooms and decided they might be good to eat.

"How do you know if these are fit to eat?" I asked Wilfred.

"You boil them with a silver quarter," he answered.

"What does that do?" I asked rather confused.

"I'm not sure," he said, "but if it turns color, we won't eat them." In actuality, he knew they were an edible variety.

We boiled the mushrooms and added them to some fish broth, attained by boiling another fish we'd brought in with our willow poles. We added the last of our flour to the mixture and had thick gravy fit for a king to go with our banic.

As if our cup was suddenly overflowing with blessings, Wilfred looked out of the tent from where we were eating and saw a fully grown mallard bobbing quietly at the water's edge. Lying down and taking aim, he shot another meal. Come morning, we'd also find a rabbit in one of our snares.

It was as if we had emerged from the wilderness into a dreamland where everything went well. We were clean, our gear was dry, and we had fresh meat once again on our menu. Then coming down the lake, we heard the echo of a Cessna engine. I ran for the signal blankets and got them spread in plain view on the sandy shore while Wilfred smothered our blazing campfire in a hastily picked armful of green boughs. The plane came into view, but seemed to be headed straight beyond us as if our signals had gone unnoticed. Indeed they had, until as Vern later told us, he had noticed the billows of smoke out of the corner of his eye and as they turned to investigate, spotted our bright yellow blankets.

After circling the island, the Cessna glided to a smooth landing on the water, and taxied into shore. Immediately Vern poked his head out of the door and said, "Greetings, voyageurs!"

"Boy, are we glad to see you," Wilfred and I chided together. "Until today we were running low on grub and we are nearly out of gasoline."

"Well, we didn't bring too much," said Vern, "we had to watch the weight."

He was right; they didn't bring much. Instead of ten gallons of gasoline, we got four, and instead of the list of essentials we'd requested, we got only a bare minimum of supplies—a box of rolled oats and a small box of tea. After weeks of pushing toward this cache, we were both disheartened and upset. We'd depended on Vern to meet us with the supplies we anticipated we'd need to survive, and he'd let us down. I held my tongue, but suspect my body language let Vern know I wasn't happy.

Given the onset of strong winds, the plane left shortly after it had landed. Wilfred and I debated if we should try tackling the formidable waters of the lake in stormy weather. Knee Lake was a wide, long lake and the wind was churning up countless white caps. Dressed in rain gear, we determined we could manage some progress as long as we stayed within a few canoe lengths of shore and stayed to the leeward side of the islands whenever possible.

We were still in danger of running out of supplies soon, so we decided the first place to seek out was a Cree fishing camp the pilot had seen from the air. We were traveling in the general direction of the camp when we came across two older Indian fishermen standing in their large wooden scow. They were pulling in their one-hundred-yard net and tossing the fish they caught into separate wooden crates on the floor of the old boat.

"How do we find your fishing camp?" we asked. Unable to hear them, we moved in closer where we got their instructions.

"Go through the channel to your right, just behind that island in the distance," they directed.

We did as they said and shortly were tied up to a half-submerged dock of spruce poles. The camp consisted of two rustic log cabins by the water's edge and a cleared area where other Indians were living in tents. The dock could not support more than a few men, but ten children and a few adults soon collected on shore. I don't think they were used to summer visitors, especially those who arrived from the north and in a canoe resembling the birch bark freighter canoes of the fur traders. Given their limited supply of gasoline, they were not willing to sell us any fuel. They tried to help us by providing insightful information about navigating the lake's endless string of islands. Apparently we didn't listen very well.

To reach southern Knee Lake, they had told us we would have to go through a narrow channel to our left, and then we would find ourselves once again on the large open body of the lake.

We stopped on an island for lunch. Shortly after we left I said to Wilfred, "There's the narrows we're looking for," we passed through, them and just as the villagers had told us, moved onto the open lake. It was still rough, but it seemed the wind was changing direction. Soon we passed two fishermen in the distance, and I remarked to Wilfred, "That looks like the same two fishermen we talked to on the way in—they really get around." The sun was directly overhead and offered little clue as to where we were. Looking at another island covered with fish carcasses, like the one we'd stopped on for a break,

Wilfred commented, "Sure are a lot of dumping sites for fish guts around here."

We traveled on with confidence in our navigating even though we had both commented that the wind had now changed almost 180 degrees. Then at almost the same moment, Wilfred recognized the rock islands adjacent to our previous night's campsite and I noticed our old campsite on shore. We had paddled from seven in the morning until three in the afternoon and ended up back where we had started!

Not content to show no progress for the day, we immediately turned south, bouncing over the waves for another six hours. We traveled across water we'd already traversed twice that day, until we finally made camp at the narrows we thought we'd gone through around noon. As if the day hadn't dampened our spirits enough, it started to rain before camp was set up. The rain turned into an all night storm of driving rain and high winds, which held us on shore until late the next morning. We finally moved out, weaving in and out of islands seeking shelter from the wind, hoping to find the sawmill that had been mentioned by the pilot when delivering Vern and our minimal supplies. As morning turned to midday, it became less and less probable that we would find it. Knee Lake would be our home for one more night.

Once off Knee Lake, Wilfred and I had three more rapids to handle before completing our trek to Oxford House. It was a wet and miserable trip. As dusk approached, we almost stopped for the night, but Oxford House was only an hour or so away, so we decided to push on. It was perhaps the most miserable hour and a half we'd spend in the Canadian interior. By the time we landed at Oxford House, my teeth were chattering uncontrollably. My body shivered both inside and out as if I was having continuous seizures. Wilfred was in about the same condition. Soon after we arrived, the area administrator invited us into his warm home where his wife presented us with a warm meal and hot tea. I finally got into some dry clothes and took an antibiotic from our first aide kit to ward off sickness. I knew we had been foolish to push on in such miserable conditions; I should have learned that lesson from my Eskimo companions. I vowed never again would I allow my partner or myself to get into that kind of situation.

The next day, Wilfred, who had agreed to travel only as far as Oxford House, bid me farewell. "Dirty devil," he said. "Good luck, but I think you've got her licked now."

I responded in another of his familiar sayings, "Affirmative, sir. I think we've got it licked now too. Thanks so much for your help."

Vern had left word with the administrator at Oxford House that he'd still not located an Eskimo to complete the trip to the Gulf with me. Given that Wilfred was now gone, I was to find another temporary partner who would travel at least to Norway House, about a four-day journey.

My new companion and guide was a Cree named Thompson Wood. He was thirty-seven years old, tall and muscular. He was in need of a haircut and missing a thumb due to a saw accident at God's River Lodge. Thompson gave me his qualifications as a guide: he was a trapper in the Knee Lake area, chewed but didn't smoke, and never drank until drunk on the job. With such qualifications, I could hardly turn him down!

As if our theme song was still "They called the Wind Mariah," we found only rough water as we splashed the length of Oxford Lake. Given the weather, it seemed appropriate when I found one of our first campsites would be on Windy Lake.

Thompson Wood and I would not be challenged by many rapids, but we would face some monster portages. For example, we had a mile-long portage between Max Lake and Logan Lake. The portage trail itself was merely a narrow footpath that twisted through the rocky terrain and climbed sharply over a towering hill for more than half its length. Wood showed me what a real voyageur was, reminding me a great deal of the early fur traders I'd read about before ever leaving home. The fur traders had carried three sixty-pound bundles of fur on their backs at each portage. Wood and I carried 160 pounds, or the equivalent of my own body weight! First we loaded Wood up, placing a heavy pack on his back with a heavy tumpline placed across his forehead; the weight pulled his head back. Then another pack was placed across the tumpline in the hollow between his neck and the backpack. This helped to straighten his head to a normal position, but when the final pack was secured on the top of his head with the pack resting on his neck, he was pitched forward. Wood and I found, as the voyageurs had, that this position made a slow trot with your load more comfortable than walking as the leaning burden of packs forced one to move forward to stay upright.

Once loaded, Wood headed up the hill and I loaded up in a similar manner. Like stout mules, we plodded nonstop across the portage. The tumpline soon tired my neck muscles from the constant strain; my eyes burned as sweat and insect repellent found a channel through my eyebrows and into my eyes. There was no easy way of doing a portage in this country. They were often hard to find, and crossing them could be a grueling experience.

Unloading one's own packs was an art. Bending slowly to a knee, like a weight lifter, I took the top most pack and swung it over my head to the ground. Then sliding the one from my neck off to one side, I firmly gripped it and twisted it to my front where I could set it down. Then I slowly slid my arms out of the shoulder straps of my backpack. Wiping the sweat from my forehead, I went back across the portage with Wood to get *Little Eric.*

We had no carrying yoke, so pulling the canoe up on shore, Wood started to lash our two paddles between the middle two thwarts. "Haven't done this in a long time," he said, as he skillfully continued to fasten the paddles in place. He wrapped my wool shirt about his neck and had me aid him in lifting the 160-pound canoe unto his shoulders. Shifting the canoe in search of a good pivot point, he finally had me let go of the canoe and started the uphill climb. He carried it to nearly the crest of the hill and then stopped while I helped him out of the carrying yoke. Once freed of his burden, Wood held the canoe as I padded my own shoulders and prepared to take the canoe. As I shouldered the unbalanced weight, it felt as if it would forever crease my collarbone. My sense of balance was off, and I tipped forward with the canoe. I started to stumble on the slippery trail. I knew I couldn't regain my balance, so I dropped to my knees bruising and cutting them on the sharp rocks. The maneuver was painful but had saved me from stretching my neck! Wood helped me back under the canoe and I again shifted it from point-to-point more aware of the importance of having the canoe well balanced. *Little Eric* was horribly heavy, and I hadn't gone far before my legs actually ached. *Man, I'd like to get out of here,* I thought. I couldn't though, not until Wood helped me, and he offered no assistance until I ended the portage at the shores of Logan Lake. I was tired and stiff but glad that we had both carried our weight for the entire portage.

Once on Logan Lake, we met four college fellows, a treat for me as I'd not seen anyone near my own age since York Factory. The four were doing some geological work for Canadian Nickel. Other than the pilot who flew them in supplies, they hadn't seen anyone for two months. In a chorus of voices, they showered us with greetings, questions, and an invitation to dinner: "Boy, are we glad to see you!" ..."Can we make you some coffee or tea?" ..."Where are you all headed to?" ..."How about some cake or even some pizza?" ..."Have you seen anybody?" We took them up on the offer for some tea, had a good chat, always a welcomed change of pace in the middle of nowhere. Then we left them to their research and continued on our journey to Robinson Portage, the longest and most historically significant portage we would encounter on our voyage.

Robinson Portage had played a key role during the height of the fur-trading era. The Hudson Bay Company had built primitive track for hand-powered railroad flatbed cars across the one-and-a-half-mile portage. The heavy wooden carts with small iron wheels had been loaded with supplies and canoes, and then pulled by hand across the portage by voyageurs. During the busy season, as many as twenty canoes and York Boats had waited at the portage to use the carts. Demand for the carts and the race to get furs to York Factory became so great that only those carrying furs for the Hudson Bay Company were allowed to use them. It gave them advantage over competing furriers. As the days of the fur trade ended, the Canadian government had taken over the track, and it eventually had been handed over to the Indians. With lack of use, it fell into disrepair, although Thompson Wood claimed some Indians were still using the track as late as 1940.

Now the fairly flat portage lay in a tangle of brush, but all three carts and most of the twisted iron and rotting wood of the track was still plainly visible. For the second time in a day, we marched across a long portage under the pressure of a heavy load. In near darkness, we packed everything across Robinson Portage except *Little Eric*. We would return for the canoe in the morning.

Darkness and heavy rain began to fall as we cooked our evening meal and we ate by candlelight as we huddled in the tent. We had crossed five small portages that day as well as two larger ones, so it took very little coaxing to put our tired bodies to sleep after dinner.

The next morning we went back for the canoe, and Wood and I again traded places partway through the portage. Although neither of us claimed to be stiff, we agreed that the canoe seemed to have gained twenty pounds overnight. When our equipment was reloaded and tied down, we pushed out into Robinson Lake. Again the wind created choppy waters and large waves for us to splash over.

On the last day of July, we rolled across Painted Stone Portage, where the Echimanish River meets the Hayes. The Echimanish River was the smallest river I'd encountered thus far during the trek. It was weedy, narrow, deep, and full of leeches, lily pads, swamp grasses, otter runs, and beaver signs. Its banks were densely covered with small willows offering no place to camp.

To keep the Echimanish River deep, the voyageurs had joined the beaver in constructing a couple of dams of fallen trees, brush, and sod. The first dam we crossed, which was still holding back water as it had for years, was selected as our campsite. This was not because it was an excellent location, but because rain threatened again and this was the first site with potential we'd seen in hours. For the second night in a row, we made camp in the rain but it stopped before we turned in for the evening. Wood and I put out a gill net in hopes of catching some fish. As we turned in, a lone loon flew by just above the trees crying his mournful tune. "He says it will be windy tomorrow," said Wood. I didn't really know if he understood the loon's call, but guessing the next day would be windy was a pretty safe bet.

The morning came very wet and very windy. I immediately thought of what Wood had said about the loon. Despite the weather, we made our way through Hairy Lake to the swift waters of the Nelson River. We inched toward the beautiful Sea River Falls where the Nelson River tumbles seven feet and wildly churns the river below. We chose to land on a rift of rock, which separated the larger falls from a smaller one. We quickly realized that the route we had chosen to our landing site was a poor one. The bank was too high, which meant it would be difficult to land quickly and get out of the current. We also found the smaller falls and the larger one fell closer together than it had appeared. They faced each other at almost a right angle, and the current pulled us in every direction. The kicker was giving ground; it could not power us through the current, and we were at great risk of being swept into the falls. With my heart racing, I grabbed a paddle and frantically paddled for the rock ledge we hoped to land on. The rumbling water made verbal communication impossible from one end of the canoe to the other. I was hardly in a position to turn and look at Wood, so I battled on in hopes that my actions were working with and not against his efforts. We knew the turbulent waters could turn us over or send us downstream in a sideways position where our craft would bear the brunt of a losing encounter with the rocks.

Once near shore, I grabbed the bowline of the canoe and quickly stepped into the swirling waters, anchoring my feet behind a rock. The current pushed the stern in close to shore, and we were able to climb up on the bank. It had been another close escape.

The portage to the head of the falls was a short one, and a welcome one, for of the 3,000 miles of water remaining between *Little Eric* and the Gulf, Sea River Falls was to be the last major portage I would make with the exception of the portage at the Continental Divide in Brown's Valley, Minnesota.

To reach Norway House, we slowly moved through the rough waters of Little Playgreen Lake. As we paddled, I took stock of what had been accomplished to date.   I would still be bucking the current until the Continental Divide, but I couldn't help but feel relief; the hardest portion of my uphill climb was over. The expedition had beaten Hudson Bay and now we had beaten the Canadian Wilderness with its rapids, black flies, and primitive portages. The biggest threat remaining was Lake Winnipeg. Hopefully, my assessment would prove correct.

Little Eric weighed over one hundred sixty pounds.

Wilfred smoking fish on Knee Lake.

Beyond Swamp Water

"For by the grace given me I say to every one of you: Do
not think of yourself more highly than you ought, but rather
think of yourself with sober judgment, in accordance with
the measure of faith God has given you." (Romans 12:3)

Journal Excerpt: August 4, 1970

"Forced to strain musk-keg water for tea tonight…I lay on a soft carpet of moss listening to the lovely music of an extremely faint wind
and the chorus of various birds, gulls, terns, and ducks. My stomach
is full of rabbit stew and banic. It's been a good day. I pray for calmer
weather tomorrow."

It was late in the evening when we landed at Norway House.
It was a Friday and apparently the one night during the
week when no one in the village sleeps. Residents moved
boisterously around the village all night allowing Wood and I
little sleep.

The next morning Wood collected his pay and headed back
to his village with some friends that happened to be visiting relatives at Norway House. On little sleep, he started back across
the trail we'd just completed. I didn't envy him.

Vern had left word for me that he had located an Eskimo to
complete the expedition's trek to the Gulf of Mexico. However,
my new companion would not be able to join me until I was

somewhere south of Winnipeg. This meant I needed at least one more short-term travel partner. I asked all around the village before finding a man willing to go as far as Winnipeg. My new Cree companion was Sidney Osburn, a thin and gray-haired man with more than eighteen years of trapping experience. We agreed to move out as soon as the wind died down and headed up the Nelson River a few hours later. We cut over to the Jack River and continued toward Lake Winnipeg. For the first forty-five minutes, we met fishing yawls or canoes frequently, but by noon we seemed to be alone. Only our canoe and the sea gulls inhabited this part of the river.

Sidney, or Sid as he preferred to be called, and I paused on Kettle Island for a lunch of corned beef and beans he'd brought from the village. We passed the tumbled down wharf and abandoned fishing shacks of Warren's Landing. From there I got my first peek at Lake Winnipeg. It was the largest body of water I'd seen since Hudson Bay, and its thundering freshwater waves reminded me of the bay in many ways. Its color did not. The shallow water had been stirred by four days of heavy winds and the entire lake resembled a vast saucer of chocolate milk.

The bright sun was partially hazed over and seemed to warm us only when we stopped. Before striking out on the lake, we dressed in our raingear and wrapped our supplies with a tarp. Since bad winds generally seemed to be from the northwest, Sid and I had decided to take the west side of the lake, but as we approached the lake, we found the winds blowing from the southeast. So we did the opposite of what we'd planned and forced our way over the waves to the east bank.

The swells grew rapidly worse as the wind shifted more to the south; we soon found it necessary to bail every fifteen minutes. Finally we were forced to put into shore just north of Montreal Point. When we landed, much to our surprise, we met an Indian family traveling by boat on their way to Norway

House. The news they had for us was not encouraging, "Been traveling six days and wind-bound nine days so far." We hoped we would have better luck than they were having with the weather.

Given the condition of the lake water, finding drinkable water was a problem. "Water, water everywhere and not a drop to drink," I mused to myself as I dug a hole in an inland swamp and collected a pool of water. I scooped it out with my hands and strained it through my T-shirt into a large kettle. We boiled the water thoroughly before using it. It definitely had a distinctive swamp water taste, but it had to be better than drinking from Lake Winnipeg.

Back at camp, Sid said he would make us enough banic for the next day or two. It sounded like a good idea, so I started to put up our tarp to shelter the coals of our campfire. Sid said the tarp made too much noise and blocked too much wind; instead he swiftly built a windbreak from green leafy branches, which worked quietly and effectively.

To make the thin loaf of Indian bread called banic, Sid put two globs of lard about the size of a quarter into a pan with four handfuls of flour mixed with a dime-sized portion of baking powder. Taking a little of the flour into his hands at a time, he rubbed it thoroughly with the lard. Once that combination was entirely mixed, he added a half-cup of water and mixed it until he had a pile of dry, not sticky dough.

Sid then melted lard in a frying pan, coating the sides as well as the bottom with the melted grease, saving the excess. Together we patted the dough into the pan as if making a thick crust. Then, like a chef finishing a prized dish, Sid took a fork and filled the dough with holes to act as a vent and ensure the inside got cooked all the way through.

Digging a slight trough in the hot coals from our fire, Sid placed the open pan on the coals. He'd wait until a golden brown spot appeared on the bread and then turned the pan to a new position. As a grand finale, he turned the banic over in the pan to brown the other side. It was the best tasting banic I'd had, but perhaps that was because I was beginning to understand the art it took to create it.

My watch had stopped working weeks ago. Our only way of telling time was by the position of the sun. Sid and I got up at what we assumed was around six o'clock. After enjoying a breakfast of rabbit from our snare, we waited once again for the lake to calm so we could depart. As noon approached, we noticed our stranded neighbors had left and decided that if they felt they could travel, so could we. The challenge we faced would be getting across the breakers and out into the deeper water and rolling swells.

Picking up all the water-soaked and slippery logs we could, Sid and I made a ramp that faced the lake and extended about four feet out into the water. We put *Little Eric* on the logs and aimed into the wind. Then we loaded up and securely tied everything down. I placed our little side-mounted kicker in an upright position, primed it, and tried the engine to make sure it would start immediately when we called upon it in the rough waters. We both removed our shoes, and rolled up our pants beyond our knees. We waited for the rhythm of the waves— slosh, slosh, whoosh, and as the next big wave swept up on shore we ran with the canoe into the muddy, choppy water. Sid kept us straight with the waves, and as soon as the prop would go down, I started the kicker. Slowly we bounced over the rough shoreline breakers without taking on a drop of water.

A few moments later, we experienced a moment of panic when we glanced back at shore and saw that our wind-bound neighbors had not left shore but merely moved their campsite to a more suitable location. Too late now—we had made it safely to deep water, and we would not turn back.

We put in a half day of very rough riding on the waves before I said, "Sid, it's time to beach."

"How do you know?" he asked.

"Because I'm bailing two to five gallons of water every fifteen minutes or so," I responded, and with that we headed in. Approaching the shore was as tricky as leaving it had been. Of the two methods of landing, bow first or sideways, Sid and I both preferred to come in bow first. We rode the waves in like a surfer, using our body weight to keep the canoe stable. Once in shallow water, we both jumped from the canoe and made our way to the bow, pulling together until the entire length of the canoe sat on the safety of the sand.

After drying out and finishing up our rabbit stew and banic, we rested for nearly an hour before we headed out onto the waves again. We used a similar type of start, but compared to our morning launch, this one was not nearly as smooth. A large wave spilled more than twenty-five gallons of water into the canoe. It was only with immediate reaction and some of the hardest paddling I've ever done that we managed to face the canoe directly into the wind before the waves could swamp it. With the water adding over two hundred pounds to our load, our paddles pulled us slowly toward a large rock off shore. We reached it, and pulled *Little Eric* up far enough to bail it out.

As the day continued, the lake grew calmer, and by evening we slid over only small waves. We camped that night on a small island of weathered rock painted in orange and light green mosses. It was no more than a football field in length and half as wide, covered with scattered vegetation. Sid and I agreed we were in the area of Poplar Point and we were content with the progress we'd covered given the rough weather.

We were both eager to beat the sun up the next day. We expected good weather, and we wanted to take advantage of it. We watched as the sun rose into the sky behind a fluffy cloud, sending down bright hazy rays as if the cloud itself was shining. The lake was so calm it offered a nearly perfect reflection of the shoreline.

For the first time since traveling along the sandy east bank of the lake, we hit some sections of rocky shoreline. A light rain fell much of the morning and turned the backdrop of trees into a green haze. Several times during the day, Sid and I passed buildings along the lake but met no people. The reason for all of the empty buildings we saw was the closing of commercial fishing on Lake Winnipeg due to mercury poisoning. As Sid explained it to me, it sounded like a vicious circle. Most of the Indians in the area had made a living by fishing on Lake Winnipeg, but now fishing was closed. As a result, the people had less money to buy goods from the Hudson Bay Store and were forced to eat more of the fish they were not allowed to sell to others.

We stopped at one of the deserted ports to explore. Sid showed me where they had stored the fish. Using horses to haul blocks of ice into the storehouse, they made their own natural freezers. They'd even been ingenious enough to build the horse corral over the water, which no doubt made cleaning it much easier for them—a sensible arrangement but one today's environmentalists likely wouldn't allow. Although most of the bunkhouses had broken windows and doors, the tin roofed homes were still in fair shape on the inside. A few showed signs of leakage and had warped floors; others still contained heaters and wood stoves. We were a little disappointed it was too early to stop for the night!

About thirty minutes after leaving the deserted fishing camp, we saw three people run down to the shore and wave wildly at us. We went to investigate, and before our canoe even touched the rocky shore, a middle-aged Indian fellow with a weathered face showing two or three days' growth of whiskers rattled off rapidly to Sid, "Our boat broke down, and we have been walking along the shoreline for a day and a half. The girls are mighty wet and miserable, and we're out of grub, and say, how ya fixed for tobacco?"

Two girls accompanied the man—in their early teens—they looked out from under their long dark hair with hopeful eyes. I assumed they were his daughters. After talking it over, I got out of the canoe, and we unpacked our supplies. Sid would take them back to the fishing village where they could get inside, build a fire, and dry out. We would leave them some of our grub, matches, and tea. That was about the best we could do. The man was sure someone from Poplar Point would soon come past the fishing camp. We assured him we'd call Poplar Point as soon as we reached the settlement at Beren's River, just to make sure someone came after them.

The man said, "I've got money on me, so I'll be glad to pay you—it sure hasn't been any good to us out here."

I replied, "Like you said, money isn't much good out here." It didn't seem right to accept his generous offer. I waited for over an hour for Sid to return. The waves oozing onto the shoreline resembled thick pea soup. Some areas even smelled sewer-like even though there were no homes, fishing camps, or villages in sight. Lake Winnipeg simply was not a very clean lake.

Ironically, when we reached Beren's River, we docked our rustic and weathered canoe next to the beautiful *Lord Selkirk*. The *Lord Selkirk* was the largest and most prestigious vessel on Lake Winnipeg, standing three decks high and about a hundred feet long. According to some of the passengers on the ship, it was a little after eight in the evening when we arrived. The Hudson Bay manager was kind enough to open up the bay store for us, and after we purchased some supplies and a pocket watch so we could tell time, he directed us to the mission to use their radio telephone.

The elderly priest agreed to transmit our emergency message about the stranded man and the two young girls to the chief of Poplar River as soon as possible. Out attempts to reach Vern and inform him of our progress was futile and after half an hour, we quit trying. "Best to get well out of village before dark," said Sid, "or maybe these Indians rob from us!" I found that a rather ironic and stereotypical statement given that Sid was a full-blooded Cree.

We pushed on for two hours and found an apparent paradise to camp in. It was sheltered, boasted a broad sandy beach, and had a nice flat area to put up the tent. Unfortunately, it was hot, humid, and completely still; we were uncomfortable even when lying on top of our sleeping bags. Then to add to our restlessness there was the disturbing *splotch* of green leopard frogs as they hopped into a puddle just outside the flap of our tent. It got so bad we actually lay there anticipating the next *splotch*—which continued all night!

Finally at four thirty a.m.—we knew because we had a watch now—we got up. That was apparently too early for our minds to function properly for we both poured ourselves a cup of hot water before realizing we hadn't added any tea to the pot. We had a hearty breakfast and started our travels before the sun appeared in the sky.

Much of the shore to Princess Harbor continued to be sandy beaches, but the shoreline where the village itself was located was rocky. The village's name was nicer than the village. It had a small store with a blue roof; many of its windows were boarded as if it was closed. A few occupied shacks, which appeared unfit for human occupancy, comprised the rest of Princess Harbor. We asked two Indians at the dock if the town had a radiophone. They said they didn't know but we should ask at the store. We did and a pleasant old man with a bad eye got me through to the operator in Winnipeg. The signal was weak and by the time the operator got my name right and the number I was calling, several minutes had elapsed. Vern was not at the number he had left me when I finally got through. Not knowing how or where to connect with Vern, we decided he'd have to find us! We started south again.

As we worked through the rockier, narrow portion of the lake, the water was choppy. It was encouraging to be able to see both sides of the lake at once. As we came within sight of Deer Island, we crossed a flock of thirty geese. Sid downed one and immediately began to clean it, leaving a trail of feathers behind the canoe as I continued to search among the rock islands for a suitable campsite. A supper of boiled goose, instant mashed potatoes, dry mix gravy, Saskatoon berries, and tea prompted us to name our new home Good Meal Island.

The next morning the winds were blasting us again. The winds seemed to be slowly shifting to the west, so in an effort to try to stay ahead of them, we decided to cross over to the western shore. By mid-afternoon the harsh winds had bested us. We sat wind-bound on the sandy beach of Hecla Island. We had only one long, wide sandbar to cross to get to the shelter of the western shore, but the waves beating on those shallow sands were so rough it looked like gigantic rapids. Maybe we could have made it, but the conditions were extremely bad—there was no questioning that; the risk to gain a few hours traveling time wouldn't be worth it, so we waited.

While the wind sometimes challenged us or interrupted our travel, the biggest obstacle on Lake Winnipeg was the merciless sun. My neck was ringed with water-filled blisters. My eyes hurt so badly that my vision was blurred as if I were standing in dense smoke. I examined my eyes in the reflective backside of the cheap watch I'd purchased, and they were bloodshot; more pink than white. My nose peeled constantly. Thank goodness, my fair-skinned face was covered in a thick red beard, which now extended to my chest. As we waited for the wind to die down, I went swimming three times: once to clean up, and twice to avoid the sun.

By morning, the waves had diminished to two-foot swells. Tackling such waves in a canoe would have concerned me before, but not now! We moved on. Only an hour after leaving camp, I saw a big change. The shoreline was full of people! There were cabins, homes, docks, boats, and the bodies of people sprawled out tanning on their bright beach towels. I saw more people in the next hour than I had seen in all the time since leaving the Arctic Circle in May.

Sid and I had been using only a small general map to navigate Lake Winnipeg. It wasn't clear where the Red River actually met the lake, so heading up an inlet, we suspected was the mouth of the Red River, we stopped next to three big yachts to find out. Hearing them state, "Yes, this is the Red River," sounded mighty pleasing to our ears! I felt like screaming, "Thank God, we've made it!" for in my own mind, I felt that once off Lake Winnipeg we were through the most dangerous parts of our journey: Hudson Bay, Hayes River, and now Lake Winnipeg, all lay behind us.

The yachters, members of the Redboine Boating Club, took an active interest in our peculiar craft and asked endless questions about the expedition. They took so many photos that Sid and I started to feel like celebrities. One of the club members insisted that we sign and trade him the paddle Wilfred had chopped with a hatchet from a wind-fallen spruce tree, for a much lighter and streamlined paddle he had on his boat. It seemed like the trade was in our favor, so we happily accepted the offer.

We finally broke away from our new fan club and continued up the smooth, languid Red River. The tall green grasses that covered both shorelines sheltered numerous bright yellow signs saying: Game Bird Reserve—No Firearms Allowed. The sign seemed fitting to us, for once off Lake Winnipeg our bent-barreled gun called Opportunity, our snares, and our fishing lines could be retired. Our living off the land was over!

The short gap between twilight and darkness was quickly closing, so Sid and I started to search among the farm fields and inhabited shore for a place to put up for the night. We spotted a beautiful huge stone church with a flat, grassy graveyard and decided to ask if we could camp there among the tombstones. At least here the neighbors would be quiet! I climbed the bank, and much to my surprise found the church was actually a museum. The structure had been erected in 1838 and still stood much as it had for over the past century. It had a huge black woodstove filling much of the center aisle and a nine-inch stovepipe running down the aisle at head level all the way to the chancel area, where it ascended through the roof. With no one around to grant us permission to stay, we moved across the river to St. John's Boys' Camp, where we were gladly invited to stay. As we unloaded, two young chaps about my own age sped up the river in a speedboat.

"There's an old man by the name of Schield looking for you," they yelled to the long-bearded fellow from St. John's who was helping us unload.

"No, he's not," I hollered back. "He's looking for me!" I got in their boat, and they raced me upstream to a campground where, sure enough, I saw the Komatik secured to the top of Vern's car. Then, as we came closer, my heart gave an extra leap of excitement, for entirely to my surprise, my folks were there too! We had nearly spent the night camped only a mile apart, but with my mother's promise of a home-cooked meal, I went back to help Sid pack everything back up and move a mile upstream.

Eureka was Barry's home for five months.

Sid making banic.

The Waterless River

"…'Everyone who drinks this water will be thirsty again, but whoever drinks the water I give him will never thirst. Indeed, the water I give him will become in him a spring of water welling up to eternal life.'" (John 4:13–14)

Journal Excerpt: August 12, 1970

"Heat is unbearable and we are perpetually thirsty. It is hard to avoid a headache when in the heat this long. My neck is blistered; sheets of tissue-paper like skin are peeling off my nose. My eyes are tender and bloodshot and my vision is blurred. Hope we get relief soon."

The next day started painfully for me as my father disinfected a needle, broke the blisters on my neck and back, and splashed alcohol-based shaving lotion on them to keep them from becoming infected. Eventually the sting of the treatment subsided and the rest of the day was much more enjoyable without the sausage-sized blisters rubbing against the neck of the T-shirt I wore to avoid further sunburn.

Vern had made arrangements for us to stop further up river at the historic site of Lower Fort Gary—a large fenced in complex of red-roofed stone buildings and well-kept grounds crawling with tourists! We portaged *Little Eric* up the hill to the fort, and placed it in a position of honor, next to one of the few remaining York boats. As I looked at the heavily constructed boat once crewed by eight to sixteen oarsmen, it was hard to imagine that it too had been transported across the very same portages we'd had to negotiate with *Little Eric.*

After so much solitude in the Arctic and the Canadian wilderness, it was a little intimidating to be in the spotlight before so many people. However, mingled with my discomfort was an intense excitement to be with people again. After answering a long list of spectator questions, we launched out on the river for a new experience, the St. Andrew's Lock, the first of twenty-eight locks we'd have to pass through en-route to the Gulf. We entered the huge rust-colored gates of the lock just as the *Paddle Princess* was leaving. Over the *Princess'* loudspeaker we heard: "If you look to your left, you'll see two fellows headed by canoe from the Arctic Circle to the Gulf of Mexico." It seemed odd at the time, as it was the first time I'd heard someone else talking about the expedition as a fact. Vern and I had talked about what the Schield Expedition hoped to do—travel by water from the Arctic to the Gulf—but now others were talking about what we'd accomplished and mentioned, with confidence rather than skepticism, the approaching end of our historic journey. I couldn't help but smile.

Sid and I carefully worked the canoe past the wake of the *Paddle Princess* and entered the lock where we were dropped a thick yellow rope and told to hang on. Then the large doors slowly clamped shut and water rushed into our closed container from upstream. We felt like a small minnow in a ten-gallon tank. Twelve minutes later, they opened the upstream gates and we were at the same water level as the upstream portion of the Red River. Before freeing us from the lock, I was instructed to come ashore and fill out a lock form. It was filled out as follows:

Date	License	Skipper	Type of Craft
9-Aug	None	Barry Lane	Canoe
Pt.of Departure	**Pt. of Destination**		
Arctic Circle	Gulf of Mexico		

Looking over the requested information, the lockmaster smiled and stated, "We don't have too many of your type run through here. Good luck. I see you still have a long ways to travel."

Our next stop was a fabulous little riverside place known as Dunlop's Museum. After hearing a bit of our journey, Mr. Dunlop termed it fascinating and offered to stuff Sid and me so he could keep us at the museum! Somehow that offer didn't sound too inviting, so after being treated to a refreshing drink, we moved on toward another yacht club that had granted Vern permission to have us set up camp on the club's property. About a mile from the club, a luxurious yacht, the *Carlabob,* met us and joining its captain on deck was Vern, his wife, Marjorie, and my parents. As we pulled into the dock, whistles were blown and a bottle of champagne was broken out. We were only given three-fourths of a glass, however, because the captain said, "Your work isn't done yet, but here's a toast to your success thus far." One swallow of champagne told me I wasn't partial to it, but Sid and I both found a great deal of enjoyment in eating the ice they had used to chill the bottle.

Everyone at the club was extremely friendly, and they rolled out the red carpet for us, a treatment which felt rather lavish after months of roughing it in the tundra and the bush. As we prepared to put up our tent on the yacht club lawn, Sid observed all the activity around us and said, "I'd just as soon camp on an island." My thoughts mirrored his exactly, but at least I had another chance to visit with my parents.

Just before turning in, I saw two young men paddle by in a canoe and not trusting their unkempt appearance, I moved our gear up the bank closer to our tent. When I thought about it, I realized those fellows probably didn't look as hippie-like and untrustworthy as I did! I mused to myself that traveling through populated areas was going to have its own challenges and surprises.

Per Vern's arrangements, the next two days were spent doing radio and television broadcasts, newspaper interviews, and making token appearances at dinners and luncheons. I found myself torn between the pleasure of being made to feel important and the tension of being forced into a role I didn't want to embrace right now. Over three months in the wilderness had brought about a change in me. The river routes of the North American continent had become my home, and my life's goal centered only on accomplishing what we'd set out to do. I no longer cared about the interviews and had little desire to leave the quiet of the river for the bustling concrete world of the cities. Talking to the media was something I'd agreed to do before starting on the Schield Expedition, and while my heart and spirit never left the banks of the river, I found myself in the city fulfilling my commitments.

Sid had fulfilled his agreement to travel Lake Winnipeg with me, and he returned to his village at Norway House. Vern let me know that Sammy Pokeelo Berthe, my new Eskimo partner, would not be able to join me for at least another week. With this knowledge in mind, I began the next leg of my journey south with a very special partner... my father!

My folks had taken their vacation to come meet the expedition at Winnipeg. My father had the time off, and I had an extra paddle. It took little prompting to get him to accept my invitation. With a smile, my mother said, "It's bad enough that I had one of you to worry about—now I've got two of you!"

On August 12, Dad and I headed up the languid Red River after bidding goodbye to my mother who was headed home. Perhaps she was the brave one. She was driving home alone in a stick shift pick-up with a truck camper. She rarely drove a stick shift and wasn't used to driving with a wide heavy truck camper. We'd likely worry about her as much as she'd worry about us!

The perfectly still water of the Red River was too muddy to cast a reflection, and in the misty hours of the morning, the river was void of any boat traffic. Dad and I thought we could make the border at Emerson in one day's travel, but toward noon we came across a grizzled old fellow in suspenders who was running a ferry across the river. "How far to Emerson?" we shouted. "About fifty-two miles by land, but about 120 miles the way you are traveling. This river twists and turns like a cork-screw." He had to be wrong we thought, but by the end of a fourteen-hour day we were ready to believe him.

The Red River didn't present the types of danger encountered previously on the expedition, but it wasn't without its problems. In fact it posed three very menacing issues. The first was the heat that had already blistered my nose and roasted the flesh on my neck. My leathery face was white only around my forehead where I pulled down my soiled and permanently wrinkled hat to shield my eyes from the sun. Even keeping hats over our eyes didn't keep us from getting headaches from the sun.

We took our feet out of the cheap knee-high black rubber boots we'd purchased. We needed the boots to trudge across the muddy banks of the river when making or breaking camp. We'd dangle our bare feet over the gunwale of the canoe, one foot dragging in the water on each side, to stay cool. With cupped hands we continuously soaked our pants and shirts, letting the wet material cling to us and provide temporary relief from the heat. Giving little thought to the danger of shrinkage, we dunked our hats and then put them back on, gladly letting the small beads of dirty river water stream across our faces and trickle down our necks. Despite these efforts, the sun drained our energy quickly. By early afternoon, we were forced to stop, seek shelter, and rest in the shade of the willows lining the bank. We stayed hidden until the sun had dipped low into the sky, and then we pushed on until darkness overcame us.

The second major problem had to do with the lack of available drinking water. The Red River didn't look clean enough to inspire us to swim in it, let alone drink it. Parched by the heat, we didn't dare use river water to quench our thirst. This was one of the gifts we had gained by entering the civilized world, I thought—polluted water. We had started the day with over two gallons of water and six cans of 7-Up, but by early afternoon we had only one good-sized cup of lukewarm water left.

We traveled for more than four hours without drinking a drop of water. We finally came within walking distance of the little town of Patterson, its name printed in large bold letters on the town's grain elevator, which could be seen from the river. I wandered into town muddy, sweaty, and well lubricated, from my hourly bath in sunscreen. As I hiked down Main Street, I felt like people were looking at me and thinking, "Look at that dirty useless hippie." I got a fellow to sell me five gallons of gasoline and some oil for our outboard, and then I went next door and bought a case of chilled pop from the hotel. I asked the woman waiting on me if I could fill our thermal water cooler, and she not only filled it, but added what ice she had, a gesture appreciated far more than she could possibly imagine.

A half-dozen elderly gentlemen patrolled the hotel steps and I could see them watching in wonderment as to how I was going to carry five gallons of gasoline, two and a half gallons of water, a case of pop, and some oil by myself. Without giving it much thought, I removed my belt and stuck my hunting knife in my back pocket. Then I tied one end of my belt to the water jug, and the other end to the gas can, and put the belt across the back of my neck. I then placed the oil on top of the pop, picked it up, and headed to the river. As I did, I heard one of the men say, "Guess he knows his business."

When I reached the bridge, both my father and I immediately downed two cans of pop. It had to be the best I've ever tasted. We'd given up hopes of reaching the border, but pushed on in hopes of finding a good campsite, which brought us to the third big problem of traveling the Red River, the shoreline.

With the river at such a low ebb each night before camping we had twenty feet of thick, grease-like clay mixture to portage across and it was by far one of the most unpleasant tasks of this portion of the journey. As soon as you stepped from the canoe, the mud sucked at your boot, and if you were fortunate enough to get it back out, the size of your boot increased with each step as more and more mud clung to its surface. If the mud pulled your boot off, your hands and arms were coated up to your armpit by the time you managed to find and retrieve the boot.

With nothing to lean on, we walked across the mud like we were toddlers just learning how to walk. Bending forward to prevent yourself from falling was futile for you'd sink in mud up to your elbow. Regardless of how we tried getting to shore, gooey mud covered much of our bodies and supplies by the time the task was done. Mud got in our pockets, plugged up our ears, smeared across our sweating foreheads, and got caked into our hair. To make matters worse, the mud stubbornly resisted any effort to wash it off.

Although we were traveling through populated areas now, camping in farmland had its drawbacks. Some of the domesticated animals we were now seeing, such as cows, took a great deal of pleasure in milling around our tent and attempting to use it as an overgrown salt lick. One night as we were sleeping, a herd of over forty Black Angus surrounded our salty tent. We had to get up and create a mini-stampede to chase them away before the herd inadvertently trampled us! Before going back to bed, we built a log and brush coral around the tent in case the cattle returned.

Ever since my father had joined me, we'd been looking for the border crossing. After two full days of travel, we still hadn't crossed it to our knowledge. Coming across a lone fisherman on the bank, we paddled over to him to ask him the location of Emerson. "It's about twenty-two miles north," he responded, "Next town you'll come near is Drayton."

"You mean we're over the border?" I inquired rather hesitantly.

"Yup—by about twenty miles," he responded.

"This here is Dakota."

"Then what's that bank," I asked, pointing across the river.

"That's Minnesota," he yelled, as we allowed the current to pull us away.

Dad and I were flabbergasted! Somehow we had unknowingly slipped across the border, and to top it off, we had spent the previous night camped in my home state of Minnesota without even realizing it. *What a quiet homecoming that was,* I mused.

At Drayton we came to a dam that crossed the river. Everything had to be unloaded from the canoe and dragged up a steep bank of dry clay and loose rocks. It took two trips each for gear, and then we returned to wrestle with our mud-covered canoe. The incline was too steep for one man to carry the canoe, and the marble-like rocks made the footing unstable. I carefully lifted the mud-caked lower end of the canoe to my shoulder, leaving me looking like a grease-covered mechanic. Dad pulled on the bow from the top of the embankment. We managed to get the canoe up the bank, and at the head of the dam we reloaded, and I showed Dad the method Wilfred had taught me for launching upstream after portaging around a waterfall, or in this case a dam.

It was wise to start the engine to make sure it was going to run and not die once you pushed off from shore and into the swift water. To avoid this, the stern man held up the running engine, and the bowman pushed off and started to paddle in a single motion. As Wilfred had so pointedly told me on the Hayes River, "Push us out easy, but hard enough; get in fast, and then paddle like the devil was after ya."

Since leaving Winnipeg, a daily sight along the Red River was the rusty and bright-colored piles of trash strewn over the banks and into the river at nearly every farm and town site. "Gee," I told Dad sarcastically while looking at one of the stockpiles of garbage, "it's good to be back with civilized people again!"

About two and a half hours south of Oslo, Dad and I stopped on a sandbar on the Minnesota side of the river. It turned out to be more than just a tea stop; the exposed river bottom we'd landed on appeared to be a graveyard! Bones were strewn across the top of the ground. Anywhere you kicked into the dirt caused another bone to appear. The bones seemed abnormal, for they were extremely large. Many of the bones were fossilized and although they resembled cow bones, backbones ten inches in diameter made us positive this wasn't the case. Later samples of those bones were identified as ancient bison by the Gustavus Adolphus College geology department.

Our next destination was River Side Park at Grand Forks, North Dakota. We landed straight across the river from a big pipe spewing yellow-green water of questionable purity into the river. I couldn't help but shake my head and wonder what we were doing to our environment. The Red River runs north, and I was starting to understand the contamination of Lake Winnipeg. As we portaged up the bank to the shady well-kept grounds of the city park, each carrying a towering pile of equipment, we encountered an elderly man and young boy heading out to do some fishing.

"You boys sure carry big loads," observed the man. I hadn't given it much thought, but I guess he was right. It's not too common to pack around something that weighs as much as you do. As I was portaging *Little Eric* past the twosome, the youngster eyed my weathered appearance and heavily bearded face.

"Mister," he finally asked, "how old are you?"

Resting one end of the canoe on the ground, I responded, "How old do you think I am?"

After brief reflection the boy guessed, "Sixty-nine!" Given that I was only nineteen years old, I could only assume that months on the trail had taken their toll on my appearance. We all had a good laugh over the disparity between my real age and his honest guess.

My mom again made the solo trip across the state of Minnesota to meet and pick up my dad in Grand Forks. This time she drove the family car with the automatic. My dad's tenure with me had been short, and while the conditions had been absolutely miserable, I thoroughly enjoyed his company. It was a unique opportunity to share even a small portion of this trek with my father.

My new companion, Sammy Pookelo Berthe, was slight of frame, spoke English well, and had more formal education than my previous Eskimo companions. He preferred to be called Sammy, but I suspected Vern would always refer to him by his Eskimo name, Pookelo. Sammy had been trained as a barber. *Good,* I thought, *now I can get a haircut. I wonder how handy he is with a hunting knife…* Sammy would eventually complete the trip to the Gulf of Mexico with me and become a lifelong friend. However, our relationship didn't start off in a very positive manner. His first words to me were, "I came to have fun and meet American girls." Obviously, he had some misconceptions about what the trip was going to involve. The faulty expectations he arrived with were also evident by his chosen attire; he was wearing dress slacks and shoes. I started to wonder what Vern had told him to entice him to sign on for this trip.

Once back on the Red River, Sammy got his first taste of reality. Although anemic compared to the Hayes, the Red River current continually flows *down north,* and we were still going uphill. By the time we stopped for the night Sammy was sweaty and dirty—and he hadn't even encountered our nightly walk through the mud yet! At least our campsite was nice. We landed at a spot where the full moon beamed down on a beautiful ripe grain field. I pretty much set up camp and made dinner by myself that evening, and Sammy and I didn't talk a lot. I could tell he was processing what he'd gotten himself into, and I gave him the space to figure things out. Perhaps that evening was a divinely planned respite, for the next two days we met only trouble.

Sammy and I still weren't talking much, and we definitely weren't working together as partners. The water was getting extremely low, and the river had narrowed to no more than forty feet in width. At these shallow spots, I would get out and walk with the canoe, but Sammy would sit in the back and uselessly push with his paddle. Near the end of his second day, we hit an extremely shallow area. When it became evident that even his own slight body weight wasn't going to allow the canoe to float, Sammy threw his paddle unto the bottom of the canoe and stepped into the water with me. Trudging along with the canoe, I heard him mutter, "Oh heck, so what if it isn't all fun and girls." When he got out of the canoe and into the mud, I smiled. I knew I had a partner—not a tourist.

From the time we rounded the first corner of the river early the next morning, we had problems. The water was so shallow that only the very end of the canoe blade submerged before hitting the bottom. The kicker and gasoline we carried became nothing but dead weight. A dozen times brush or muddy dikes blocked almost the entire width of the waterway. Often large portions of the clam-studded river bottom were entirely exposed and bone dry. We eventually learned that the Red River was as low as it had ever been since records were kept. During spring floods, this area of the river was sometimes nearly ten miles wide—hard to believe given that its entire span was now only a few feet wide and no more than a foot in depth.

We soon discovered we were not the only ones struggling with the Red River mud and drought conditions. We came across a helpless spring lamb buried belly deep in the clay. It had likely been drawn to the river for a drink and got mired in the mud. Unable to free itself, and exhausted from its struggle, it lay helpless. Sammy and I stopped and struggled through the mud to save it. We carried it to the top of the bank and left the tired creature in some shade, hoping it would regain enough strength to walk again. Our rescue efforts had brightened our day.

Later the same day, we came across a huge sow pig also apparently struggling to survive as it lay helplessly paralyzed in the clay mud. All we could see of the sinking bulk were the nostrils of its huge blunted nose, the bent ears, and a small portion of its back. Realizing the financial investment some farmer had put into that pig, we decided to crawl the bank and go tell the farmer he was losing one of his pigs. Once we crawled up the bank, we found a pasture full of monstrous pigs separating us from the nearby farm; we decided the risk of walking across the field wasn't worth it. After a short debate, we agreed it would be a restless night's sleep if we didn't attempt some sort of rescue, so we devised a plan. The pig was too big to lift, so we found a stout prying pole. Admittedly proud of our humanitarian efforts, we staggered and crawled through knee-deep mud to the pig, where we were met with an unhappy grunt. We were shocked when the pig easily stood up and walked to shore. With gapping mouths and embarrassed expressions we returned to *Little Eric,* grateful we hadn't gone to the farmer with our concern for his wallowing pig! He'd have had a good laugh regarding our naïve concern over a pig stuck in the mud.

We met some fishermen along the river, but for the distance we traveled, it was really very few. Most of our river companions were farm animals, and Sammy and I became true experts at imitating cows, pigs, sheep, and ducks. At night we were serenaded by crickets and frogs, and despite the fact that we were traveling through the heart of a well-populated area, we typically found ourselves in seclusion on the river. The late August weather continued to be unmercifully hot and dry; water levels continued to drop. Out of the last ten miles of river we'd traveled, we had to pole the canoe six miles. We walked four miles and at one point even had to cut a path through trees that had fallen across the river.

We connected with Vern again at Fort Abercrombie. Whenever we met Vern, he always arranged for the press to be there. Sammy liked being in the limelight. That evening Sammy told me he had fallen in love with the college girl who had interviewed us for the paper. I ribbed him that the heat was getting to him, but he seemed sincere, so I didn't pester him too much. Perhaps he could be a voyageur and meet the American girls he wanted.

Each day we faced blistering sun for twelve hours in miserably low water and with barely enough to drink. At night we almost collapsed. The fact that little Sammy had taken the same beating I had increased my respect for him greatly.

When we reached Breckenridge, Sammy and I saw a two-day dream come true. We both took a nice long shower at the motel where Vern was staying and feasted on the biggest bowl of ice cream we could find. Following the usual newspaper and radio interviews, I told Vern we were having a great deal of trouble navigating the river. "I want you to keep pushing until you run out of water," Vern said, and with that, Sammy and I returned to the river.

Five miles south of Wahpeton, North Dakota, the river went from extremely low to entirely dry. Sammy and I literally set up camp on the waterless, weedless riverbed, and walked to a nearby farm. From there I called Vern and informed him that we had indeed followed the Red River to its final drop of water. I had been told the river was waterless for the next twenty-five miles.

The farmer was kind and generous. He offered to let us stay at his place, feeding us breakfast the following morning. He and his boys returned to the river with us and helped carry our gear to the edge of one of his fields. *Little Eric* was loaded onto a farm truck to be transported to the nearest water. It was heartbreaking in a way but another whim of nature we had to accept. Vern met us for this highly unusual portage and captured it on film. We bounced for twenty miles in the back of the farm truck to the White Rock Dam, where we once again had navigable water. It was already late afternoon, so Sammy and I traveled only as far as Reservation Dam where we made camp in the dark and enjoyed one of our special dinners of canned corned beef and beans mixed and warmed together.

After the short portage over a highway at Reservation Dam, we reached Lake Traverse and the best travel conditions for the expedition since early August. I had a few solid goals set in my mind from the beginning of the Schield Expedition. One was to always be moving south, another milestone I had anxiously been waiting for was the continental divide. This was where we would end our long pull uphill against the current and at last be going down south with the flow of the water. That marker of our progress was at Brown's Valley, Minnesota, located two hundred miles south of the American-Canadian border. It is here that the raindrops split, some going down north, others going down south. Here we would make our final portage in the remaining 2,200 miles to the Gulf—a one-mile portage down a black top highway!

A large crowd of people met us as we came off Lake Traverse, but it was the completion of the portage that made Sammy and me happy. Many people insisted on lending a helping hand, greatly lightening our loads. Sammy and I and a host of other would-be voyageurs followed a police escort down the highway to the Little Minnesota River. We had crossed the continental divide! Once we entered the Little Minnesota River, we went only a short ways downstream and landed at Sam Brown City Park. The rest of the day and a good portion of the night, the park was like a fairground. The whole town seemed to have turned out to take a look at *those nuts canoeing from the Arctic.* We were photographed far too many times, answered a steady stream of questions, and according to Sammy, we met many beautiful American women.

Next morning, *Little Eric* was again placed on a truck for a five-mile ride beyond un-navigable water to Big Stone Lake. With ease, we pushed on to Ortonville where we were met by more people, and with happiness and glee, I announced to the newspaper reporters, "From now on, it's downhill all the way." In one sense, I couldn't have been more mistaken.

Barry's dad joins him on the Red River.

The Red River goes dry.

Happiness Runs in a
Circular Motion

*"Give thanks in all circumstances, for this is God's will for
you in Christ Jesus." (I Thessalonians 5:18)*

Journal Excerpt: August 27, 1970

"Felt as happy as a kid with a popsicle after portaging across the continental divide. For the first time in over three months we will be going
south with the current."

The Minnesota River flows south, the same direction
Sammy and I were traveling; however, low water and
a forest of fallen trees almost made it impossible to
navigate. Forty years before Sammy and I traversed this section
of the Minnesota River, Eric Severaid and Walter Porter had
canoed it en-route from St. Paul to the now abandoned settlement of York Factory. Judging from the condition of the river,
it appeared no one had canoed it in the forty years between our
two trips! When we left Ortonville, Minnesota, we told Vern
we'd meet him that evening at Appleton—a small town just
down river. It was two and a half days later before we finally
arrived!

The river twisted and turned between two steep banks

making hope of going ashore to portage around an obstruction a difficult task. Dikes of trees dammed the river in numerous places; brush, sand, and smaller branches piled against fallen trees forming solid barriers that often stretched from one side of the river to the other. Many of the trees had twelve- to fourteen-inch trunks and cutting our way over, under, or around the mountains of waterlogged wood was a Herculean task. Doing what we could with only a hatchet and a hand saw, Sammy and I slowly made our way south, quite literally, inch by inch. At one point Sammy mused, "I think I've cut more brush than I have hair." That was a significant statement given his profession as a barber!

As if river conditions weren't enough to keep us occupied, *Little Eric* added to our difficulties when the fiberglass, worn paper thin in places, started to separate. We had a half-inch-wide, eighteen-inch-long hole in the bottom center portion of the stern.

Sanding it off as best we could with a tattered piece of wet sandpaper, river sand, and my knife blade, Sammy and I soaked gauze bandages from our first aid kit in fiberglass patching material, and used the strips to plug the hole. It wasn't a pretty patch, but we were confident it would hold for at least a few days.

Some good came out of those miserable miles on the Minnesota River; it strengthened the friendship between Sammy and me. We faced and conquered some tremendous challenges together. I think we grinned simultaneously when we emerged from the narrow portion of the upper Minnesota River onto Marsh Lake. Shortly thereafter we connected with Vern. While Sammy and I had been wrestling with the conditions on the river, Vern had been getting anxious. He couldn't imagine what could be detaining us while paddling through Minnesota farmland on a small river. Much to our pleasure and surprise Vern had brought along some of his friends and some fresh steaks for a shore lunch. Vern's friends had a daughter about our age, and Sammy promptly fell in love—again. I was beginning to suspect this would be a recurring event!

After discussing it with Vern, we decided to travel as far as Montevideo, Minnesota. We'd stop there long enough to get *Little Eric*'s fiberglass hull repaired. Now that I no longer had to carry the canoe over portages, I didn't mind a few added pounds of weight. At Montevideo we made arrangements to take *Little Eric* into town for repairs. Sammy and I camped out in the city park and spent our time talking to people about our adventures. When news spread that we were ready to get back on the river, a crowd from the community gathered to see us off. Once *Little Eric* was loaded, I thought we were ready to go, but Sammy said, "Just a minute," and scrambled up the bank, and rubbed noses with one of the girls!

He smirked, "I couldn't help it; I fell in love again." As we pushed offshore, dozens of cameras aimed at us seemed to go off simultaneously with one loud click. We rounded the bend, and once again we were alone with nature.

We encountered several sand and rock bars just south of Montevideo, but the water was deeper and we were able to maneuver around them. Sammy and I had changed into clean, dry clothes during our last stop, but their comfort and pleasant smell were short lived. The first of September, our first full day of travel since leaving Montevideo, dawned with a stiff all day downpour. By the time we broke camp, the sand bar we had called home for the night was barely large enough for the tent; the water was on the rise. We had to bail twenty gallons of water from the canoe before we could pack it. It was no pleasure to be wet, but we were glad to see the rain.

We worked our way through a small rapid an hour later and paddled into Granite Falls, Minnesota. Here a man offered his assistance in portaging *Little Eric* across two manmade dams a short distance apart. We loaded our gear and then *Little Eric* into his pickup, but the canoe stuck out so far I had to hold it up and trot along behind the truck. It was easier than carrying everything, but I was grateful I was in good physical shape and had been a cross-country runner! It was at Granite Falls that Sammy and I sensed a real change; beyond that point the river became deeper and sand bars fewer.

We zipped through the ripples of Patterson Rapids and camped just beyond the babbling noises. We looked up at the star-studded sky and listened to the crackle of the fire and the sizzle of frying catfish some friendly fisherman had given us. It seemed to me like I could let out my breath a little. At the little town of Morton, I got a call through to my folks. I had always told them things were going well, but this time I felt better about it because I knew it was really true. Surely we were beyond the danger and hardship we had struggled through on almost a daily basis.

Unlike the Red River, the Minnesota River channel was predictable. It didn't meander aimlessly from one side of the river to the other. It always followed the steeper bank and the outer corner of bends in the river. In the rapids you were safe to assume that a V-shaped area of smooth water meant a rock-free place to shoot the rapids. We traveled for days hitting only two rough patches. We had to pull *Little Eric* over a single log in the first situation and on another occasion slid precariously over a hidden rock in the swift current. Once I was nearly beheaded by a low hanging branch but quick reactions saved me from what could have been at the least a very sore neck and a likely headache.

The weather was starting to change. Small fleets of autumn yellow and red leaves filled the air and floated downstream with us, reminding us that our only race now was with the weather. A gray squirrel busy preparing for winter scampered up a tree branch and scolded us for disturbing his work. In striking contrast to the severe heat and drought conditions we'd endured on the Red River, mornings and evenings were getting cooler, and it now seemed like it rained nearly every day.

We dodged showers by taking shelter under bridges when we needed a break. The rising water was swallowing up the sandbars and flat beaches near the river making camping sites difficult to locate. One evening somewhere downriver from New Ulm, we failed to find a campsite before dark. The skies suddenly opened up on us; rain falling in heavy non-stop waves. We made straight for shore, and in a well-practiced routine soon had our tent, "Eureka," up with our gear inside, and the canoe tied. With the rhythmic downpour beating relentlessly on the tent roof, we opted for a cold supper of corned beef and an apple.

The college I attended, Gustavus Adolphus College in St. Peter, Minnesota, is located near the Minnesota River. I was looking forward to reaching that milestone. It would be wonderful to see the friends that had given me such a heartfelt send off nearly five months earlier. I wanted to give them each a big burly hug and thank them for their prayers. The river miles between Mankato and St. Peter couldn't pass fast enough until Sammy and I noticed something we couldn't resist. There, sitting by the highway but also right on the river was a Dairy Queen store! Our mode of travel didn't call for a great deal of money, so our first problem was finding enough cash to buy any sort of ice cream treat. By thoroughly rummaging through our packs and belongings we managed to pull together nearly five dollars. Sammy, in his haste to beat me to the store, failed to slip back into his shoes, and after he had imbedded several sharp sand burrs into his foot, had me carry him piggyback to the service window and then back to the canoe. If sweet treats can qualify as a memorable event, those were perhaps the best tasting and most memorable ice cream cones we had ever eaten.

We reached St. Peter, and for the next two days, both the college and the community treated the Schield Expedition royally. More than fifty students from the college, plus professors and townspeople, met us at the St. Peter Bridge where we received a formal welcome from the mayor. *Little Eric* was loaded on a trailer along with Sammy and me, and we were given a police escort through downtown St. Peter and up the hill to the Gustavus campus. As we were parading through town, Sammy said, "There are a lot of pretty girls here." I had a feeling he was going to fall in love—again.

Ma Young, the wonderful woman that managed the college food service, prepared steaks for what she called the Barry Lane Canoe Banquet. The college president, many of my college professors, some of the city fathers, the mayor, and the chamber of commerce president, the captain of the police force, my parents, and Vern were all there. Sammy and I were asked to say a few words, and then we were each awarded a college jacket. Sammy remarked, "If I ever have any children, I'll send them to Gustavus Adolphus."

Following an interview, Sammy and I went outside for a host of pictures and set up living quarters on the college mall. "Gustavus' first sleep-in for the season," chuckled President Barth, "and I'm in no hurry to see a second—at least this one is legal."

On the evening of September 5, goodbyes to friends and my folks were said again, but this time they didn't seem so hard. Everyone said goodbye with confidence that we would be seeing each other again before too long. When I had left in May, some had seriously questioned that I would ever return. Early the next morning, one of the college faculty showed up with a trailer and we piled everything on it. We went down the St.

Peter hill to the river with Sammy and me on top and astride *Little Eric* as if riding a horse. With only a few there to bid us farewell, we returned to the solitude of the river.

The risks of traveling on the Minnesota River were minuscule compared to the Arctic or wilderness areas already conquered. Perhaps that made us complacent. We soon discovered we could never let down our guard. Content to let the canoe drift with the current, *Little Eric* rammed a submerged log, hitting it just off center enough to tip the canoe on its side. Overreacting to the tipping, I jumped to the other side of the canoe and splashed with a gasp into the chilly September water. The canoe was half filled with water, and part of our supplies dotted the river's surface and floated away, however we had not tipped over. I hung onto the bow until Sammy had bailed the canoe. Then he paddled to shore and built a fire, dried off, and made a steaming cup of tea. Given that our drinking water was one of the items we'd lost when the canoe tipped, we were forced to use river water, which turned a sewer-water gray after we boiled it. Reluctantly, we drank it anyway.

The Minnesota River flows into the Mississippi River, and that was our next milestone. Once on the mighty Mississippi, we would be on the homestretch to the Gulf of Mexico. It was hard to comprehend that the full length of the Mississippi River from Minneapolis, Minnesota, to the Gulf of Mexico at New Orleans was less than a third of the total distance the expedition would travel.

No bands were there to greet us, but we were jubilant. We had reached the Mississippi! Now in the twin cities of Minneapolis-St. Paul, Sammy and I found ourselves canoeing between tall buildings that bordered the river. The shady and forested banks we were accustomed to were replaced by a skyline of cement and concrete levies. *Little Eric* was no longer king of the river, his twenty-foot length soon dwarfed by the tugs pushing their heavy rust-colored barges. The solitude we had known so long on the river was disrupted by yachts, speedboats, paddle wheel excursions, and houseboats. Even the fresh air of the country was stifled by the heavier acrid smell of a big city.

Welcome to civilization, I thought. I was now looking forward to the end of the expedition, not because I didn't enjoy the voyageur's lifestyle, but I wanted to get down the polluted Mississippi as quickly as possible. I soon found, however, that my impressions of the Mississippi were as wrong as some of the stereotypes I'd had of the Eskimos.

Between major cities on the Mississippi, such as Minneapolis-St. Paul, St. Louis, Vicksburg, and New Orleans, the river stretches through uninhabited forested beauty as it has for hundreds of years. Both banks are often outlined with wide sandy beaches and ample supplies of driftwood, making scenery enjoyable and camping a breeze. Once beyond the boundaries of a city, river traffic diminished to only a dozen barges or so a day and a few yachts. Other than that, Sammy and I once again rode the river alone. Bridges were few and far between, being found only near the big cities. Only the locks slowed our steady progress downstream.

At Hastings, Minnesota, Sammy and I pulled *Little Eric* up on shore and hiked a mile into town for supplies and for a newspaper interview Vern had arranged. When we returned to the river, a light rain began to fall. With black clouds coming in swiftly, Sammy and I pulled *Little Eric* under a willow tree. We fashioned our ponchos into a lean-to type shelter. Sammy rounded up three semi-dried logs for our shelter; one to act as a table and two for chairs. I built a small fire. Building a fire from all hardwood isn't easy, and along the river that was all we could find. It was doubly hard when all the wood was wet, so I put to use some of the expertise garnered from my time with Thompson Wood earlier in the voyage. He had told me, "When it rains, all wood gets saturated except dead, standing willow. It stays very dry." He had also told me, "In rainy weather when you need to strike a match, bend over and strike it on your zipper." Applying this knowledge, Sammy and I were soon sitting in a semi-dry shelter with a nice little fire.

We had reacted to the weather none-to-soon, for dark clouds quickly overtook us, and the wind-driven rain hammered our flapping ponchos like hail for the better part of an hour. By late afternoon, our rain gear was as wet inside as it was outside. We were drenched to the skin. Even though it was still raining steadily, once the lightning stopped we packed up and moved out. Our rainy progress was slowed at the next lock. As we approached, we saw a red traffic light, meaning we needed to stay out of the approach way for the lock was already in use. A tug and nine rusty barges of coal were slowly being winched to the upper level of the river. Forty-five minutes elapsed before the big orange doors of the lock opened and a whistle was blown signaling the barge to leave. With its diesel engines throbbing, the craft inched its way past us and on upstream.

Little Eric looked out of place in the six hundred-foot-long lock. It was incredible to believe that well over two million gallons of water were being brought in just to give *Little Eric* a free ride to the next level of the river. Following the lockmaster's directions, Sammy and I maneuvered about halfway through the lock, where we pulled over to the cement wall and waited to be thrown some lines to hang onto. We needed the lines so we would not aimlessly drift about in the lock's massive space. By now, Sammy and I had learned that our lifejackets made good bumpers between the canoe's wooden gunwale and the slimy cement walls of the lock. With the bumpers in place and the long yellow ropes dropped to us, we waited for the huge doors to close and for our twelve-minute drop to the lower portion of the river.

"Say, I heard about you fellas," said the friendly lock worker who had dropped us the rope. "Must have been some trip," he added.

"Ya, it was," Sammy and I chimed.

"Looks like you boys are in for some more rain," he continued.

"Just what we need," I said, grinning through my water-soaked beard.

Finally the whistle signaling our departure was blown, and we moved out through the steady drizzle. Our next stop was to be a city park in Red Wing, Minnesota, where Vern had told us to stop for a newspaper interview. There our gloomy day took a turn for the better. We met some men working on a pipeline, and they asked us to join them for an evening barbecue. We had been planning on eating Ramen noodles we'd been carrying around with us since Fargo, so a juicy steak sounded awfully good! It was only four p.m. and still raining; with the barbecue not until six p.m., we had plenty of time to set up our camp. We had just made ourselves comfortable inside our tent and were trying to warm our little shelter with a candle when a deep male voice just outside our door asked, "Anyone in there?"

"Yes," I responded. "Just a minute."

As I zipped open the tent flap, the first thing I saw was a pair of polished black shoes. I was quite sure what the rest of the uniform would look like. It was a Red Wing policeman. Someone had phoned in that a couple of hippies were setting up a camp at the city park! Thus our prompt visit from the local police force; fortunately for Sammy and me, the man was very pleasant. And after we explained to him who we were, he said he'd go explain the situation to the person that had called in and we were not to worry about things unless he returned.

When the officer left, Sammy asked, "Do you really think

he bought our story? I mean, canoeing from the Arctic to the Gulf doesn't sound too realistic."

"I guess we'll know if he comes back," I replied. When it came time to leave for the barbecue, the officer hadn't returned, so we made our way to dinner and had a wonderful time. The steaks were tender and the size of a dinner plate, served with baked potatoes and juicy tomatoes. Much better fare than Ramen noodles!

More than comfortably stuffed with food, Sammy and I headed back to our tent. The evening was calm and, at least for the moment, rainless. With such favorable conditions, we decided to break camp and tackle Lake Pepin. We had been told over and over again that we'd have to be luckier than most to cross that lake and find it calm. One old fellow said, "That lake ain't calm all day, and not many times at night...seems to be in its best mood during late evening or early morning." Well, it was definitely late evening when Sammy and I reached the lake, but too late to be to our advantage. Lake Pepin appeared to be tranquil, but with overcast skies, darkness quickly enveloped us. We hung close to the shore searching for a place to camp, but the only level spots we found were lawns in front of lake homes and cabins. Offered no other alternative, we finally beached our canoe in front of a cabin. The cabin was dark, so we left a note on the front door. It read, *"Traveling by canoe and needed a place to camp, hope its o.k. Sammy Pookelo Berthe and Barry Lane."* Hoping no one would show up at the cabin that evening, we set up camp on their lawn.

It was fortunate we'd stopped when we did. It rained extremely hard most of the night, and by morning both of us were wet—especially Sammy, as the pole-bending wind had blown the wet wall of the tent tight against his sleeping bag. He was upset. Sammy had wanted to face the tent in the opposite direction but had given in to me. I confessed I had misjudged the wind, but added it was only my *second mistake* of the year.

"On top of that," Sammy said, "in the middle of the night, I wanted to put a pack against the tent to hold it away from my sleeping bag but you sat up and said to leave it alone and go to sleep!" I protested, for if I had said that, I must have been sound asleep at the time. Sammy and I continued ribbing one another as we packed.

As we feared, Lake Pepin was no longer sleeping when dawn came. It was covered with white-capped waves two and a half to three feet high. The wind was out of the northwest. That was good; it meant the wind would be at our back. We pushed off boldly. We used our little kicker, both to make better time and as a safety factor against the waves and undercurrent created by passing barges. As we progressed down Lake Pepin, we hit a submerged log and broke our sheer-off pin, so we were forced to paddle to shore. Landing in white water is never easy, or dry, and that morning was no exception. Shallow water forced me to jump from the canoe. By the time the canoe was safely pulled into shore, I was drenched. While I steadied the canoe, Sammy replaced the pin. We battled with our paddles to get back to deep water, only to find that Sammy had assembled it incorrectly and we'd already lost our new pin. We went through another wet landing.

Sammy ribbed me, "I can't figure out how I did that. Oh well, it's only my second mistake of this year!" Back on the rough water, conditions still weren't pleasant. Sammy accidentally dropped his lifejacket overboard, and in the rough waves, it took us nearly half an hour to circle back and recover it. Snatching it from the waves, Sammy smiled, "Would you believe that's my second mistake this year?" We both grinned.

A stop at Lake City, Minnesota, added a little sunlight to what had started as another dreary day. Sammy and I staggered up to a food market to buy a few supplies, and when the price was rung up, we found ourselves a quarter short. I promised I'd run down to the canoe and get more change if she'd trust us. The lady waiting on us said she would, and we took our goods and went to the canoe. Sammy went back up with the quarter we owed and returned with a folded piece of paper. "She handed me this," said Sammy. We opened it and found a dollar and a note: *Send me some post cards. Mrs. Eldon Steffenhagen.* We were still cold and wet on the outside, but such friendship and hospitality made us feel great.

Since we'd left Minneapolis-St. Paul, calm water and clear weather had been nearly nonexistent. Ironic, I thought, within weeks we'd gone from severe drought to near flood conditions. Regardless of what the weather did, I couldn't help but notice the towering hills along the river. They were cloaked in forest green occasionally broken up by the sheer bare face of yellow or orange sand and limestone cliffs. The dark forest shadows, the tints of autumn leaves, and the patches of open sandy beaches created a picture of unmarred beauty. I was wrong in my prejudgment of what the Mississippi River portion of the expedition would be like. Without question, it was beautiful. I often felt like I'd been dropped into a Mark Twain novel.

When we stopped at La Crosse, Wisconsin, for a newspaper interview, we met the captain of the *LaCrosse Queen,* a paddle wheel excursion ship. The captain's name was Roy Franz, and he took a deep interest in the expedition. He fixed us some lemonade, let us use his phone to call Vern, and then took Sammy uptown for two and a half gallons of gasoline, which he insisted on paying for. I think part of that was the good Lord's doing, as we needed gas desperately and were out of money. Sammy observed, "You know, most people have sure been nice to us." I had to agree.

The weather we were encountering wasn't nearly as nice as

the people. Pounding rains hammered us relentlessly day and night. Somewhere near the city of Genoa, we were dealing with both rain and wind. The waves were no larger than many we'd bounced across, but these waves were steep, sharp, and came in close rhythm that offered the canoe no chance to roll over them. *Little Eric* slapped over each wave like a stiff board. Sammy, in the bow, bit his paddle into the crest of the waves, but his efforts seemed futile, as we could not avoid taking on water. Two wind-blown waves broke over the bow and into the canoe. Sammy and I both swallowed hard—in an instant we'd taken on so much water we were in definite danger of going down. With Sammy paddling and me bailing and running the engine, we inched toward shore. If there were angels assigned to watch over us, they were doing their job—we landed safely. With taut nerves and wet, tired bodies, we made camp among the willows. We were now approximately 1,400 miles north of New Orleans, our final destination. If the rains continued, it was obvious that portion of the trip wasn't going to be as easy as we had anticipated. In the dull, flickering light of a candle, Sammy and I lay listening to the music of the crickets and the occasional snaps of our dying fire. "You know, Sammy," I said thoughtfully, "it wasn't such a bad day. We moved south."

Up to this point we had kept our gear reasonably dry by wrapping it in king-sized garbage bags, but Sammy and I had been getting soaked. Our ponchos were so saturated they'd essentially become useless. We decided that garbage bags might provide better shelter from the ongoing rain. We made a slit in the bottom of the bag for our heads and poked an arm out each side. We were quite a spectacle in our green, knee-length bags, but by day's end they had proven their worth. We were wet only from our knees down and on our arms.

After going through our ninth lock, we pushed on to Battle Island, just beyond Victory, Wisconsin. We stopped to call Vern and let him know our location. The people running a small odds and ends store at Battle Island noticed we were cold, and the lady soon appeared with two hot cups of coffee. Their hospitality was warming, and they took immediate interest not only in our trip, but in our comfort. "Feel free to take any canned goods you might need," they said. "There will be no charge." We took nothing but a second cup of coffee and thanked them.

A few days later, Sammy and I met up with a couple of elderly men named Scrap and Sam. They were out fishing and beckoned us over when they saw *Little Eric.* They'd been hearing about our adventure on the news, and they had a thousand questions. Scrap said, "Say, you'll be around Lancing by noon; Sam and I will meet you at the DX sign for lunch." We agreed, and they left us in the wake of their boat. At noon, while it continued pouring rain outside, Sammy and I found ourselves sitting in a warm, dry cabin enjoying our second barbequed steak of the week, with Scrap, Sam, and their wives. We were surprised to learn that the two men were old acquaintances of Vern Schield. They had actually helped him design and build some of his early rock quarry equipment. Grateful for their hospitality and shelter from the heavy noon downpour, Sammy and I donned our garbage bags and prepared to head south.

"Where ya figure to put in tonight?" asked Scrap.

"Near McGregor, Iowa," I replied.

"Maybe we'll drive down and see if we can find ya," he said.

Scrap and Sam showed up with their wives that evening and provided us with dinner. Turns out McGregor was the closest we'd come to Vern's hometown of Waverly, Iowa, and Vern had arranged a celebration for the next day. Numerous friends of Vern planned to attend. Ralph Frese, maker of *Little Eric,* and three men dressed in voyageur attire drove down from Chicago to see us. Frese was a fascinating man who knew canoes and the history of the voyageurs better than most. He was, of course, full of questions about my evaluation of *Little Eric.*

"To be honest," I told him, "it was worthless on the bay, but a fine river canoe." This, of course, prompted more questions, and all I could think was, *Gee, I wish I'd spent a week with this guy before we ever started the expedition.*

Given that the events of the day had kept us in town, I ended the evening with a phone call home, which lifted my spirits considerably. Sammy decided to make his own phone call. He called one of the girls he had fallen so madly in love with during our trek through Minnesota. We returned to our camp two happy voyageurs.

"Sammy," I said, "the only thing that could make life better now is decent weather."

"Amen," said Sammy.

Little Eric in the locke.

Little Eric needs repairs.

Gee, People Are Nice

"God is our refuge and strength, an ever-present help in trouble." (Psalms 46:1)

Journal Except: September 25, 1970

"Given the flooding, the Mississippi River is especially dangerous and dirty now, but the people we meet and the river scenery daily surpass my expectations. I'm enjoying myself, but am ever so anxious to be done."

The Mississippi River is part of the largest river system in North America and is the second longest river in the United States. It starts out as a small stream in northern Minnesota that one can literally step across and becomes deep and wide enough for ocean liners by the time it hits the delta near Baton Rouge, Louisiana. We would be on the Mississippi for nearly 2,000 miles, and we learned its currents and sheer size made it a dangerous place for small craft such as a canoe. To complicate matters, it had now been raining day and night for over a week. While fall floods on the Mississippi are a rarity, Sammy and I were starting to feel like Noah must have felt, watching the rain come down around the ark. The river was swelling rapidly, and we were shooting downstream with increasing speed accompanied by masses of flood debris. While we had no way to accurately gauge our true drift speed, my best guess was that we'd increased from three miles an hour to seven; in areas where flooded tributaries or other rivers flowed into the Mississippi, we went even faster.

When we arrived at the Dubuque lock the lockmaster said he had a message for us. We were to meet Vern at the yacht marina. By the time we reached the marina, Sammy was chilled. We climbed the rain-soaked hill but found no Vern. Deciding we'd better wait, we both crammed into a phone booth to get out of the rain. "Now I know how a sardine feels," I told Sammy. We started lighting matches in an effort to warm our cramped enclosure. For two hours we waited, but no Vern. Finally, we called the police, but no accidents had been reported. Bewildered as to where Vern could be, we crossed the river and made camp. Our first aim was to get some warm tea into Sammy. The dry roots from fallen trees aided us in starting a fire; after some tea, pork chops, and soup, Sammy finally stopped shivering.

We put on the driest clothes we had, slid into our makeshift garbage bag rain gear, and canoed back to the marina; still no Vern.

"He's bound to be in town somewhere," said Sammy.

"That's true," I agreed. "Let's call a cab and see if we can spot his car." We hailed a cab, but before it arrived, the city police came to investigate some suspicious looking characters reported to be hanging around the yacht marina…possibly vandalizing the phone booth! He graciously listened to our story and seemed content we were not a threat to local property or residents. Shortly after he left, our cab arrived.

"Where to, boys?" the cabby asked.

"Well," I said, "we're looking for a peculiar car that will probably be at one of your better motels."

"What's so peculiar about this car?" he questioned.

"It's a green Monte Carlo," said Sammy, "with a dirty, old dog sled on top of it."

"And some brightly colored signs," I added.

The driver called his station, "Check and see if anybody's seen a green Monte Carlo with a dog sled and some big signs floating around the city, will ya?"

In just moments came the reply, "It's been spotted at the Holiday."

"Roger," said our driver, and we were off.

"I feel like a detective," said Sammy.

Once we reached the motel lobby, Sammy refused to go in with me. "Not the way we look," he stated. "We'll probably get thrown out." I had wondered the same thing myself, but shortly we were both knocking on Vern's door. When he opened the door he looked startled, then happy, then upset!

"For goodness' sake, I thought you drowned," he stated.

"Vern," I grinned, "you should know by now that I have a habit of turning up eventually. Where were you anyway?"

"Where was I?" he gasped. "Where were you? Why I nursed ulcers for two hours waiting for you." After more discussion, the problem became clear. We had both waited, only two hours apart as the river flows, at different marinas. After confirming arrangements for the next day's media interviews, Sammy and I headed back to our campsite.

The next morning we broke camp and moved to the yacht marina where Vern had made arrangements for TV and newspaper interviews. The TV cameraman with a heavy, expensive, camera harnessed around his neck insisted on riding in the canoe to get some close ups. I was sure we'd tip and he'd sink like a brick. Fortunately we didn't.

Sammy had developed a severe cold from his chill the previous day. Given that he was not feeling well, I suggested he ride with Vern in his car to the next town and I'd reconnect with him there. It would have given him at least one day out of the cold rainy weather that perpetually plagued us.

"Not on your life," he said stubbornly. "If you go on the river, I go with you. We're partners, remember?" While I continued to be concerned for his health, it made me feel good when he said that. It had taken us a while, but Sammy and I had grown to be good friends and partners. We had become like brothers. Together I was confident we could tackle the worsening conditions on the Mississippi.

As we progressed south on the river, we met more and more barges. Their foaming wake typically created only minimal problems as the waves they created spread out across the river. However, on one occasion we met a large tug pushing eighteen loaded barges; we met near an island, which constricted where the waves from the wake could go. They quickly grew into tall breakers as they neared the shore of the island—where we had retreated for safety. We were battered by the waves as they hit the shallow water and were doubly surprised when the breakers rebounded off the island hitting us again. The turbulence of the waves threatened to capsize us. Given the length of both the passing barge and the island, Sammy and I struggled for ten minutes to keep *Little Eric* afloat.

By the time we made it through our twelfth lock somewhere in mid-Iowa, the rising water had tuned a muddy brown. "Sammy," I said, "I've noticed two things about the shoreline lately."

"What's that?" he inquired.

"For one thing," I said, "the hills are starting to disappear and the land is flattening out."

"What's the other?" he questioned.

"Well, it's just that I haven't seen an evergreen along the river since we left Minnesota."

Sammy commented, "I've noticed something lately too."

"What's that?" I asked.

"There's getting to be an awful lot of water in this river! I'd say it's a good two to three feet higher now than it was in Minneapolis."

Looking up at the cloudy sky, I added, "And it looks like it's going to get even higher."

At our fourteenth and fifteenth locks, we met a caravan of barges. We settled down at each lock for a cup of tea and waited as they winched the long line of barges through. We lost an hour at each lock. After another long wet day, we landed at Lindsay Park Marina near Davenport, Iowa. I walked up to the clubhouse to ask permission to tie up *Little Eric,* and to ask if we could put our tent up in the shelter of one of the big yacht garages. Sammy and I had already figured where we could put up the tent for the best protection from the weather. However, my asking was in vain. Dr. and Mrs. Foley, owners of the garage, recognized me when I entered the clubhouse, apparently from some news clippings, and they overhead my request. "Nonsense," said Dr. Foley. "Here," he continued, handing me a key, "you're sleeping in our yacht tonight."

Their yacht was something else. It was like an ultra modern forty-foot trailer capable of sleeping six. "It even has a flushing toilet and a hot shower," Sammy commented, "on a boat!" It was the closest thing to sleeping in a regular bed that I'd had since my stay with Hudson Bay Manager, John Wallace nearly five months earlier. It was heavenly! The best part was being able to scrub down to clean flesh, get into some dry clothes—and being able to stay that way for more than an hour!

As if their kindness hadn't already been enough, Mrs. Foley showed up bright and early the next morning with bacon and eggs for our breakfast. "I couldn't remember what we'd left on the boat to eat," she said, "so I thought I'd bring a little something down."

"How can we ever repay you?" I asked.

Smiling sweetly she replied, "Well, there is one little thing you could do."

"Oh, oh," I grinned.

She continued, "Our little son, Chris, fell in love with you rugged voyageurs when he heard your story on the news, and he would really like to have you come and talk to his third grade class."

"How about that, Sammy?" I laughed. "We're going to school for show-and-tell."

Sammy and I highlighted many of our experiences for the kids, and they listened intently—especially one little girl sitting in the front row. When we asked if they had any questions, her arm shot up immediately.

"Where did you go to the bathroom?" she asked.

Sammy looked at me and said, "You can answer this one."

I smiled at her inquiry and explained that there were no bathrooms where we'd traveled in the Arctic, so we could go anywhere. I added, "In cold weather you just don't go very often, and you do it as quickly as you can because of the cold." After our delightful time with our third grade audience, Mrs. Foley drove us back to the marina.

As we bailed *Little Eric* out and headed to midstream, I told Sammy, "This time it's my turn…Gee people are nice!"

For the tenth straight day it rained; we paddled in the minimal comfort of our garbage bags. But the rain was now affecting us with something more serious than the discomfort of wet clothing. The river had swollen tremendously, and I estimated our drift speed had increased to ten to thirteen miles an hour. We needed to constantly stay alert to the threat of big logs running downstream like battering rams and to debris that continually threatened to snap our sheer-off pins or even capsize the canoe. The current was now so strong, the red and green buoys that marked the river channel would be pulled under by the current only to rocket back to the surface without warning. It was like canoeing through a high-risk obstacle course at faster than normal speeds.

Eureka, our tent, had been set up in some rather strange places; next to railroads, on boat docks, near highways, and in city parks, but perhaps none was more unusual than our campsite in Muscatine, Iowa. We made camp on a cement slab under the balcony of a clubhouse. Like our raincoats, Eureka was saturated after ten days of rain, and it had started to leak badly the last couple of nights. We camped under the balcony to keep the tent out of the rain!

Each day conditions on the river grew worse. On September 18 when we launched out into the river, we found ourselves surrounded by a maze of sudsy foam, trees, garbage, and in one place an oil slick so thick Sammy was afraid to flick his hot cigarette ashes out of the canoe. The river was covered with a raft of junk, including barrels, lawn chairs, and garbage. Despite the mess in the river, we were happy! For the first time in nearly two weeks, we were zipping along under a cloudless blue sky in eighty-degree temperatures.

"I thought weather like this was a thing of the past," said Sammy.

"Shhh…or it might go away," I warned.

It appeared our sunny weather was going to be short lived. So at Burlington, Iowa, we made camp under a noisy highway bridge, less than a block from a railroad crossing, and only half a mile from a rowdy bar with loud music. Needless to say, we didn't get much sleep and wasted no time leaving early the next morning. The river was shrouded with dense fog; one could rarely see fifty to sixty feet. We decided to stay close to shore and only travel under paddle power until the fog lifted. However, the amount of debris near shore forced us to move out into deeper water. We soon lost sight of shore; we were traveling blind and realized we were at great risk. The morning was silent except for the gurgle of the turbulent water. Sammy and I could hear every dip we made into the river with our paddles. Then we both heard it—a steady powerful swish, swish, swish, coming at us through the fog. We knew what we heard echoing toward us was a tug pushing a raft of barges, but we couldn't tell exactly where the sound was coming from, and we could see nothing. We stopped paddling and strained our eyes in all directions. We saw nothing but dense fog and heard only the rapid pounding of our own hearts and the steady swish, swish, swish of the tug as it pushed the smooth water of the river aside with the barges. Suddenly the barges emerged from the fog, they were three abreast, and *Little Eric* was dead center of the middle barge.

"Start the engine!" I screamed at Sammy, and as he pushed our little engine to full throttle I paddled furiously. Our quick reactions were barely fast enough; we cleared the outer corner of the barges by less than a canoe length. We watched the long dark form slide by us. Eighteen barges in all. "They never would have known they hit us," said Sammy.

"Nor would anyone else," I added soberly. Turning at a right angle to the current and watching for logs, we worked our way back to the shoreline and hugged it closely the rest of the morning. The fog did not lift until almost noon.

We pushed on to Keokuk, Iowa, where we were to meet up with Vern. Some people in a large yacht met us on the river and told us where to dock *Little Eric* and how to get in touch with Vern. Only two hours later, we heard that they had hit a submerged log like those Sammy and I had been dodging. They lost their beautiful boat, and we were told that they nearly drowned.

"Maybe *Little Eric* is outclassed by all these yachts and pleasure boats," I told Sammy, "but when it comes to maneuverability in this log-infested river, we've still got ourselves the king of the river."

"I think you're right," he agreed.

At Keokuk, Sammy and I once again got the royal treatment from old friends of Vern. They opened up their home to us, and after allowing us to scrub ourselves down, took Vern and the two of us out to dinner. I leaned over and whispered to Sammy, "We used to live off the land, but now we live off the people of the land."

"I know," smiled Sammy, "but I like it. People are ... "

"I know," I cut in, and then we both laughed—"people are really nice!"

As more and more tributaries joined forces with the Mississippi, the water continued to rise. I'm not certain if the high water of 1970 was ever officially declared a flood, but I do know the water was near flood stage, and the river was as angry as I ever wanted to see it. As we paddled through some whirlpools caused by the currents, Sammy said, "That mean old Mississippi is really showing its temper again."

"At least the rain has finally stopped," I stated. In fact, it was so hot and sunny we stripped down to our waists for the first time since leaving the Red River. I burn exceptionally easily, so at the appearance of the sun, I started to grease my body with sun tan lotion. "What on earth are you doing?" I ribbed Sammy as he coated himself with sun tan oil.

"I'll be darned if I'm going home a pale Eskimo!" he joked.

It seemed like we could not string two sunny days together. Soon we were back to traveling in pouring rain. As we crossed lock twenty-five, the lockmaster said to us, "You boys look mighty miserable. There's a restaurant right on the river about a mile up that slew—might pay ya to get out of this rain and get a hot meal there." We thanked him and took his advice. We made our way to the restaurant, Stay and Play, and after four cups of steaming coffee and a big platter of fried chicken, Sammy and I felt revived. We watched the water stream off the roof of the restaurant like little waterfalls for nearly an hour, but by the time we left, we had a blue, sunny sky dotted with fluffy white clouds. It remained that way for almost two hours, until we neared Alton, Illinois. We noticed an approaching wall of dark purple clouds coming from the northwest. We were already within view of the Alton lock, and we wanted to get through it before the storm hit, so we pushed on, keeping one eye on the weather. We were less than ten minutes away from the lock when the wind started to pick up. This was a signal for us to put into shore; we did so immediately, landing in eerie darkness as the heavy clouds rolled overhead.

We quickly sprang into action. In a flash, we had the tent up and cross-tied to four big trees, our supplies thrown inside the tent, and *Little Eric* secured to a tree. Our frantic efforts took us about fifteen minutes. After tipping *Little Eric* upside down, we ran into the tent, and before we had zipped it shut, the skies ripped open. The rain beat on our canvas so fiercely that normal conversation was impossible. The place we had chosen as our campsite was a two-inch deep lake in a matter of minutes. We could feel the cold water turning the soil beneath our tent floor into soft, soggy mud. We were surrounded by flashes of lightning and loud bursts of thunder. Had *Little Eric* not been tied down securely, I'm sure it would have blown away.

We lit two candles to make Eureka cozier. Then Sammy and I shook hands, and whispered prayers of thanksgiving for being spared what could have been another miserable evening if just a few minutes had been lost. The initial fury of the storm passed in about half an hour; the rest of the night was marked by a slow, steady rain. "I wonder if ducks even like this weather?" Sammy grumbled as he crawled into his damp sleeping bag.

The last time we'd had contact with Vern, we'd agreed to meet him on the waterfront near the St. Louis Arch, the steel rainbow known as the Gateway to the West. To accommodate Vern's wishes and the press coverage, he was arranging we would arrive mid-morning on the agreed upon date. That meant Sammy and I needed to be on the very outskirts of St. Louis the night before.

Although our plan to camp near the outskirts of the city seemed sound, we soon found it was seriously flawed. The city of St. Louis and surrounding communities dominate the shoreline of the Mississippi for miles. Sammy and I had pushed too far and stayed on the river too long. As darkness started to settle in, we found ourselves amid an endless alley of industrial buildings and warehouses. Setting up camp in the warehouse district of a strange city is a vulnerable feeling, and our gut instincts were validated.

About two o'clock in the morning, someone gave our tent a violent shake and hollered, "You in the tent! Come out here!" I sat bolt upright.

I whispered to Sammy, "Get your knife—we may need them." As I unzipped the tent flap, I could see we were surrounded by a gang of African American youth. The pit of my stomach tightened. As Sammy and I crawled out and stood before them, I prayed that somehow the Lord would protect us. I counted seven as the gang moved in closer. They started talking in a fast, animated manner, and between their Southern drawl and unfamiliar lingo, I caught only bits and pieces of what they were saying. This much I figured out—they'd found our canoe and wanted to know what we were doing on their turf. By God's grace, they thought what we were doing was *cool* and *brave* and above all they were fascinated that Sammy was a "*real Eskimo.*" They wanted to know if he lived in an igloo, rubbed noses, and ate whale blubber. They peppered us with questions for two hours. Finally, they told us to go back in the tent and get some rest; they would stay and protect us and our belongings from the potential risk of another gang or vagrants that inhabited the waterfront area.

As we crawled back into the tent, I thought, *Lord, you do have a sense of humor; instead of being attacked by a gang, here they are guarding us from other intruders.*

Sammy asked, "Are those guys American?"

"Sure," I said.

"Then how come they hardly speak English?" Sammy inquired.

I chuckled as I answered, "Given that we are now in the South, we may both have problems understanding what others say."

Sammy and I were up by six o'clock the next morning. It appeared most of our guardian angels were gone. Ali, the apparent gang leader, and a couple of others were still there. Ali was perched on a fifty-gallon barrel and leaning against the wall of a nearby warehouse. After a brief conversation, he and the others started to leave.

Ali hollered back over his shoulder, "Take care of yourselves. Next time we won't be there to save your sorry butts!" He was right, this time we had been fortunate and blessed, but I vowed to myself we'd never find ourselves in that situation again if it could be avoided; there would be no more camping along the waterfront of a major city.

When Sammy and I landed near the St. Louis Arch, we had no idea we were going to be taking on a first mate—especially one that was only seven years old! When Vern had first posted an ad looking for someone to lead the Schield Canoe

Expedition from the Arctic to the Gulf, one of the applicants was little Thomas Dean from Cedar Rapids, Iowa.

Part of Tom's letter read: *"I'm smart and strong and don't take up much room. I have all the equipment that is needed including food, clothes, fishing tackle, and hatchet. I have done a lot of camping."*

Well, Tom didn't get the job he wanted, but given the youngster's interest in the expedition, Vern had invited his father to drive him down to St. Louis to meet us.

Tom was a yardstick and a half high, had light sandy hair, and a toothy smile. He was not easily intimidated. After months on the water, I was a muscular 170 pounds with a full-bearded face, a sunburned nose, and a weathered unkempt look; I looked like something out of a mountain man movie. Sammy was still a primitive Eskimo to those who didn't know him. Our unsightly appearance didn't dampen the enthusiasm of young Thomas Dean.

"Can I ride to New Orleans with you guys?" he bluntly asked.

"What about school?" I questioned.

After a brief moment of thought, he suggested, "Once we get on the river, I don't think my teacher could find us."

"But you don't have any equipment." Sammy said.

Tom smiled and looked down, "I brought my own paddle and life jacket just…just in case."

Sammy and I were smitten with our sandy-haired little friend. Taking a youngster out on the Mississippi in the present conditions was a questionable call, but we talked to Tom's father and then to Vern, and it was agreed. Tom could ride with us from St. Louis to Cairo, Illinois—but he would eat, sleep, and travel in his life jacket!

We settled Tom in the middle of the canoe and left St. Louis around noon. Given the high water, it was getting tough to find campsites along the river. That evening was no exception; we were forced to camp in a low spot only thirty feet from the river.

Tom pitched in and helped Sammy unload the canoe and put up the tent while I mixed up some beans and corned beef for supper. As Tom crouched around the fire with us, he asked, "What's to drink?" Drink? Sammy and I looked at each other. What on earth did we have to offer a seven year old to drink?

"Looks like you'll have to drink tea like the rest of us men," I said, emphasizing the "men" in hopes it would make him want tea. "It's the best trail drink there is."

"Tea it is," Tom said. But as Sammy and I watched him take his first swallow, his facial expression betrayed his distaste. "That's pretty good," he said. But Sammy and I doubted his sincerity. Our first mate peppered us with questions and told us stories until the embers of the fire started to die down. We turned in, but our sleep wouldn't last long. Around one in the morning, I was awakened by the soft lap of waves only inches from the tent. The river was still rising and it was about to overtake our campsite. We had no time to pack neatly; we flopped everything, including sleepy little Tom into the canoe. Our situation wasn't good, and now I was having second thoughts about being responsible for young Tom. The only guide we had through the inky blackness were some lights we'd spotted on the other side of the Mississippi. They were apparently on top of some on-land oil tanks, likely located on higher ground. I held my breath all the way across the debris-cluttered and unpredictable river, but nothing disastrous happened and we were soon stumbling through a brushy trail to a small clearing.

Tom never uttered a word of complaint, but helped Sammy mop out our wet tent and soon was back in his sleeping bag curled up and asleep. Like an alarm clock set to go off at 7:00 a.m., we were rattled awake by a train rolling down a track only twenty-five feet behind the tent. Such a startled awakening brings one around quickly, and soon we were back on the river.

By this time the Mississippi was a solid blanket of dead trees, parts of buildings, pieces of boat docks, balls, vegetables, and even a dead pig I pointed out to Tom. "Looks like he's doing the back stroke," Tom joked. Unable to escape the debris, we lost four sheer-off pins by noon. Later that afternoon we put into shore for lunch and to replace a fouled spark plug. More or less to give him something to do, I pushed the bow of the canoe partway into the river and asked Tom to hold the bowline while I worked on the engine.

"There, that should do it," I said, snapping the cover back on.

"How do I get in?" asked Tom.

"Oh, just walk across the water," I said sarcastically. But when we were ready to go, Tom was in the canoe and wet up beyond his knees!

Ending 104 miles of travel that day, we landed at Trail of Tears Campground, where our motley crew of three received a lot of interest from other campers. We told them of our troubles with the rising water, and they told us that they had heard the river was supposed to crest at thirty-four feet in the next couple of days. One unanticipated benefit of the rising water, we were making incredible time. I'd been told a raindrop that falls into the river at the Mississippi headwaters makes it to the Gulf in ninety days. Based on that, I'd anticipated it would take about six weeks to canoe to New Orleans from Minneapolis-St. Paul. At the rate we were now going, we were likely to shave two to three weeks off that anticipated timetable!

Less than ten minutes after leaving Trail of Tears Park the next morning, a few sprinkles started to fall, and Tom became our boy in a garbage bag. Tying him securely in his lifejacket, Sammy and I slid Tom into a garbage bag with a slit large enough to poke his head out. We squashed his hat down over his eyes. Two minutes after those first few drops fell; a driving rain limited our visibility. The downpour lasted forty-five minutes before slowing to a steady, uncomfortable, soaking shower. We stayed near shore to avoid barges we weren't sure we would be able to see. Sammy and I both worried about how Tom was going to handle things, but our stout little voyageur never complained.

Sammy was in the stern running the kicker as it gave us more control in the swift, log-infested water. He made a sharp turn to avoid a log and the handle broke off the engine, slipped from his hand and quickly disappeared in the murky water. To steer, one now had to twist the entire outboard. We'd figure out something for a handle once we landed. We were only eleven miles out of Cape Giradeau, Missouri, and thought we could handle the outboard without a handle that distance. As we neared Cape Giradeau, Sammy headed for the bridge hoping it would allow us to land someplace sheltered from the pelting rain, but we found a steep wall and no landing spots. This meant turning against the stiff current and heading back to a dock we had seen up river. We had gone only the distance of a football field beyond it, but to make up that lost yardage took hard paddling and a half hour's time.

Sammy and I slipped out of our garage bag rain suits, and we all made our way to the nearest eatery, the Cowboy Café. Once in the café, we received some bewildered looks, especially Tom, as we pulled him out from under his rain-soaked hat, a garbage bag, and a life jacket. We notified Tom's folks that he wouldn't be getting into Cairo, Illinois, until the next morning and let them know that he was fine. We took time for a hot breakfast, this time offering Tom some milk to drink. "I like this better than tea," he admitted. By the time we were ready to get back on the river, the rain had stopped, and that evening we found a broad sandy beach to camp on. It was a beautiful spot and, judging from the abundance of driftwood, was apparently a spot unused by other campers. We built a roaring bonfire and left Tom with the task of feeding it driftwood while Sammy and I set up camp.

It was windy enough to tie the tent down, but after turning it 180 degrees we still had not found a suitable position. No matter which way we faced it, one of the walls always bellied in and one always bellied out. Deciding one position was as good as another we finally anchored the tent to two big logs. When we turned in, we were dry for a change and slept in comfort.

By mid-morning the next day, we reached Cairo, Illinois. Sammy and I could tell Tom was getting excited to see his family again. As we neared the park that was our rendezvous point, we could see Tom's father anxiously waiting at river's edge. Sammy and I landed the canoe parallel to the shore, as we often did in a strong current.

"How was the trip, son?" Tom's father asked.

"Fine, Dad," Tom responded as he beamed from ear to ear. A big hug followed once Tom was on shore, and then the chatter about all his heroic adventures began spilling out faster than the river current.

While we said our farewells to Tom and his father, I finished carving a wooden handle for our kicker out of a piece of dry willow I'd started working on the night before. I notched it so that one end fit into the tiller bracket on the kicker; using the point of my knife I bored a bolt hole and we secured our new tiller handle in place. With tears rolling down his cheeks, our little friend Tom stood and waved as we left Cairo. Sammy and I didn't cry, but I'm sure we both could have. We missed the little guy. Sammy even stuffed a dirty sock Tom had left behind into his pack and told me he was saving it as a souvenir. Once again Sammy had fallen in love, but this time it wasn't with an American co-ed.

Canoeing through the heartland of America.

Seven-year-old Tom joins the expedition.

At Journey's End

"I have fought the good fight, I have finished the race, I have kept the faith." (II Timothy 4:7)

Journal Entry: October 6, 1970

"I always wondered what the last night before completing this trek would be like. It's a dream like so many of the realities that have already come and gone. It is raining tonight and we've another seventy miles to canoe tomorrow. Tomorrow it's all over—the last wrung on the ladder. It seems too far away and too surreal to prevent my sleep tonight."

Once we left Cairo, we were on what is considered the lower Mississippi. Having been joined by the Missouri River just north of St. Louis and the Ohio River in Cairo, the last thousand-mile stretch of the Mississippi becomes a giant waterway, unequaled by any other American river system. The countryside along the lower Mississippi is also different. Gone were the scenic hills and bluffs that lined the river throughout much of Minnesota, Iowa, and Wisconsin. The country here was quite flat. As we surveyed the shoreline, the floodwaters often gurgled among the shoreline willows that had once been separated from the river by a broad band of golden sand. We soon encountered something we'd not previously seen. As the land flattens, the river spreads out, and manmade dikes of pilings, rock, and earth jut far out into the river. Their purpose is to keep the channel deep enough for the barges. Not needing the water depth of a barge, Sammy and I often cut across the bends in the river to save ourselves miles of travel each day.

To navigate the Mississippi, Sammy and I only carried a simple road map. *After all,* we thought, *how can one get lost on a river—simply follow the current south.* Unfortunately, Sammy and I weren't aware that the manmade dikes or wing dams existed and our road map obviously didn't show that type of detail. To make matters worse, the floodwater had submerged the wing dams from view. It was the afternoon of September 28 when we encountered the first of these dams. Up to this point, Sammy and I had been having a peaceful day on the river. I was in the bow and not paddling, as we were moving swiftly under the speed of our little engine and the force of the swift river current. The river looked fine ahead of us, and I started digging in a pack behind me in search of a wet stone to sharpen my knife and our hatchet.

Suddenly Sammy hollered, "Watch it, watch it…watch it!" I looked up at him and his frightened eyes looked as big as saucers. I turned quickly and looked downstream, where I saw the misty spray, and could now hear the rumble of a manmade waterfall. We were trapped in the draw of the dam, and we knew that to turn away from it would mean going over sideways, so we did the next best thing. We prayed and prepared to shoot the dam.

I clutched my paddle firmly, and Sammy cut the engine speed to half-throttle. We selected a place where the water flowed smoothly over the dam wall. Smooth water was an indication there were no jagged edges awaiting us, but we had no idea what we would be falling into below the dam. In a split second, we found out. *Little Eric* flew over the dam and plunged downward; below me I saw nothing but white turbulent water. I experienced an instant of sheer panic and felt as though I didn't dare breath. Everything happened so fast—yet it was like the moment was suspended in time. The bow plowed into the water, and I attacked the river with my paddle straining to pull the bow of the canoe back to the surface. I had momentarily been completely engulfed by the river. Sammy twisted and turned the engine this way and that to combat the pull of the whirlpool surrounding us. Frantically whipping my paddle from side-to-side, I bit my paddle into every wave that threatened to swamp us. We took on perhaps fifty gallons of water, but somehow we stayed upright and in one piece! With the gunwale of the canoe nearly at the same level as the water, we forced our way hastily to shore. We were shaken, but we'd managed to escape the fury of Old Man River. As we looked back at the wing dam from the down riverside, we could see we'd made a vertical drop of almost seven feet.

"You've got some gray hairs now," joked Sam.

"Ya," I kidded, "and you're the first pale Eskimo I've ever seen!" The next day we shot over three more wing dams. Fortunately, they were half the size of the first one that had surprised us. Sammy and I agreed that when we got to Memphis, we'd find a river map that showed the size and location on any upcoming dams.

I'm not sure how we settled on the subsequent plan; perhaps it was because we'd decided that until we found a map we'd follow the channel markers to avoid any additional mishaps with wing dams. Following the channel meant we were closer to the commercial barges that constantly shuttle cargo up and down the river. Sammy and I noticed that the barges threw up a wake of about eight waves, all approximately three feet high. Those waves stayed at about the same distance behind the mighty diesel tugs like they were tied to a string; we knew that they made better time going downstream than we did. The rest seemed to follow logically.

We would stay at a safe distance as the barges chugged past us, but once they had gone by, we would slide in behind them and allow the canoe to be picked up by the fifth or sixth wave back. It would tilt the canoe at a forty-five-degree angle, and we would race along wildly behind the barge. The best part was we could run our little outboard just fast enough to stay on the crest of those ever-present waves for extended periods of time. It was almost like surfing.

It was in such a wild manner, after riding a single wave for over an hour, that we came into Memphis, Tennessee. Sammy gave the kicker a little burst of speed, I paddled, and we slipped off our foamy crest into the wave trough and soon were back on our own. I'm not certain how we ever became bold enough to try it the first time, but once we found out it worked, hitchhiking on the wake of a tug headed south became a daily occurrence.

As we approached the cement levy protecting the shoreline from erosion, we asked a couple sitting on the sun-warmed cement if there was a dock somewhere nearby where we could tie up. They informed us there was one just beyond the bridge.

"Where you all from?" asked the young man.

"From the Arctic Circle," said Sammy.

With a feminine gasp, the young lady said, "You mean you came all the way in that itty bitty thing?"

Swelling to his full manly stature, Sammy simply said, "Yes."

At the bridge, we tied *Little Eric* up under an old wooden pier near Frank's Boat Store, which, like most everything else on that portion of the river, was built on a barge. The bank behind the pier was steep, and between the pier and the piling was nothing but loose rock.

"Where on earth are we going to sleep?" Sammy puzzled.

"A good question, Sammy," I replied.

"Let's ask if we can sleep on the deck of that tug," he proposed. Following his suggestion, we boarded the *Emily Jean* and introduced ourselves to the tug's engineer. We told him who we were and explained our apparent problem to him.

"Ridiculous," he said, "the deck of a tug ain't a decent place to camp. The *Emily Jean*'s been mired here for repairs, and I'm the only one on board—with four extra bunks, you two might as well make use of them." Once again Sammy and I had come into a city as haggard-looking voyageurs and had found a friend on the waterfront. We took him up on his offer.

The next morning we were awakened to one of the finest breakfasts we'd had in some time: sausage, eggs, and freshly baked bread. After breakfast Sammy and I found we had a new problem. The river current had slowed down considerably as the river had broadened, but it was still on the rise, which had caused them to move all the barges along the pier. One had been moved forward and now trapped *Little Eric* under the pier like a tiger in a cage. In order to get back on the river we had to unload all of our supplies, pull *Little Eric* out from behind the pier, and portage everything fifty yards down the bank over uneven terrain.

It was just south of Memphis that we saw a beautiful throwback to yesteryear. We'd seen many strange, large crafts on the Mississippi, but the three-deck *Delta Queen* was one of the most picturesque and magnificent sights we'd taken in. She was one of the last operating steamers on the Mississippi, a living relic of a day gone by.

"What a big boat," said Sammy. "A little bigger than us, huh?"

"No," I replied, "a *lot* bigger than us."

Now we literally seemed to be flying downstream—especially when we hitched a ride on the wake of a tug. While riding one tug's wake, we'd missed one of our connections with Vern. We were focused on the wave we were riding, and he couldn't see us from shore because of the canoe's low profile in the midst of the tug's wake. I can't say that Sammy and I missed the interviews we'd likely have been roped into had we stopped. We managed to get downstream from where Vern thought we'd be. It took him four days to catch up with us again!

Near Helena, Arkansas, even though it was now early October, the weather was beautiful. In anticipation of getting a good start the next day, Sammy and I both voted to roll out our sleeping bags and sleep under the stars. However, we spotted a big black rat just before retiring and changed our minds, quickly setting up Eureka as we normally did. Turns out rats weren't our only problem. The sand bank we had chosen to camp on was covered with tiny burrs, which not only made for uncomfortable sleeping, but made it very difficult to roll up the tent in the morning. Hundreds of the miniature pin cushions clung to the floor of the tent and threatened to make tiny holes if we rolled them up in the canvas. So one by one, we painfully pulled them out. The process took nearly an hour.

Then in our rush to get breakfast and be on our way, Sammy spilled the tea and nearly put out the fire. We rekindled it and I proceeded to pull an identical maneuver. At that we gave up the idea of breakfast and headed toward Greenville, Mississippi, where we were to meet Vern.

Greenville was not directly on the main portion of the river, but rather far up a channel. A channel which Sammy and I journeyed up for two miles before deciding it was too far out of our way. There had to be a more logical place to land and connect with Vern. We turned back toward the main stream in search of a marina where we could call Vern. The scene awaiting us at the mouth of the channel was like a highway traffic jam. In four minutes, we saw five tugs, some of them pushing as many as forty-two barges. One had just passed the mouth of the channel, churning up a hectic wake, which was rebounding off the sides of our narrow side stream. Two barges were passing just south of the channel, setting up conflicting wakes, which slapped together and spit spray high up into the air. Then to entirely surround us in confusion, a tug backed out from behind us and practically chased us into the churning water of the river ahead. The tugs' laboring at their tons of cargo had only minimal control as far as trying to turn quickly. In the powerful current and churning water, Sammy and I were more nimble—we scooted between the two barges that were meeting just south of the channel to reach less crowded water.

It soon became evident that the marina we felt sure we'd find further downstream didn't exist. We tried to head upstream again, but even with paddles and the kicker going wide open, our labors against the force of the Mississippi were futile, and it easily continued to push us south. Finally, eleven miles south of the channel that led to Greenville, Sammy and I slid to shore at the Riverside Soybean Factory on the Arkansas side of the river, and they graciously allowed us to use their phone. We called Vern to tell him what had happened to us, but he wasn't at the motel, and we later found that the message we'd left for him at the front desk did not give our location. Again we sat waiting for Vern, while he waited for us, not knowing where we were. We killed time until we could no longer stand it. We flipped a coin; Sammy lost, and started hitchhiking into Greenville to see if he could find Vern.

Vern too had grown impatient and came looking for us. About the time Sammy reached Greenville, Vern spotted the canoe and me along the river. We promptly sped back to Greenville to find Sammy. The three of us finally connected at Vern's motel. Sammy came in with a wide smile and said, "Gee,

I rode with two nice truck drivers and an attractive girl. I think I might have fallen …"

Shaking my head, but smiling, I said, "Come on, let's get back to the river."

It looked like the day would end on a happy note as we found high sandy ground for our camp that night. Both of us slept poorly because we were excited about nearing the end of the expedition. I already felt a bit sad at the thought of leaving Sammy and stepping out of *Little Eric* forever. I'd done everything to that canoe except curse it and kiss its bow. I pictured the end of the expedition with some sadness, yet felt compelled to push on; I could not rest until we'd finished what we started out to do.

In the course of the expedition, we'd had numerous brushes with potential disaster or even death, yet neither my companions nor I had met with one bad accident during the whole journey. We were always trying to spot a potential mishap before it could happen. Yet even when being careful, accidents can happen. The misfortune we didn't avoid was relatively minor. I needed to cut a piece of wire, as our homemade tiller arm was finally working loose from the bracket of our little kicker. I was going to wind the wire around the area where the tiller arm was bolted to the kicker to help reinforce the connection. I was being careful, but the wire casing I cut through contained no wire, and my knife cut through the thin, empty plastic coating much faster than I had expected. For once I was sorry I kept such a sharp edge on my knife, for it not only sliced through the empty casing, but quickly penetrated to the bone of my left hand. It didn't hurt, and for a second didn't bleed. Then the deep gash began to bleed profusely. I applied pressure and held the cut tightly shut. Sammy was more upset about the whole episode than I was, and his patch job, though efficient, made it look as through my entire hand had been mutilated.

In all sincerity he asked, "Do you think I should make a sling for your arm?" I told him I didn't think that was necessary. He treated me like a complete invalid, refusing to let me do anything all day. It was late afternoon before we reached the high cement walls of the Vicksburg, Mississippi, dike and landed behind the *Sprague,* the largest paddle wheel to ever run the Mississippi River.

Once in Vicksburg, we walked into the emergency ward of the hospital. I asked a nurse if I could see a doctor, as I'd cut myself rather badly earlier that morning. She scolded me for not coming in sooner, so Sammy and I started to explain why we were so late in coming to the hospital. Our story soon attracted quite an audience of doctors and nurses in the emergency ward. The doctor finally said, "Well, it could use some stitches, but since you've put so much antibiotic ointment on the cut, we'll just try cleaning it up and taping it for you…but try not to move it too much." We met Vern as we were coming out of the hospital exit. He looked rather nervous because all he had heard was that one of us had to go to the hospital.

With *Little Eric* under the watchful eyes of two young boys Sammy and I had hired to watch our belongings, Sammy, Vern, and I took in some of the historic sites of Vicksburg including the *Sprague.* Now retired, the fine old steamer sat moored to the Vicksburg levy as a museum. The *Sprague* was powered by the largest paddle wheel ever built, and at one time held the record for towage on the Mississippi River. Looking over the gigantic steam engine, Vern said, "I'm afraid this puts out a little more power than you boys and your paddles!" He added, "But then you've gone a lot of places it never could—guess that makes you even."

With great hesitation, Sammy and I debated where we would camp. It was always with an unsettled mind that we put up the tent on any vacant, dark, waterfront. We had vowed we wouldn't do it again after our experience in St. Louis, but out of both daylight and options, we did it again that night. We slept with one eye open but had no problems with uninvited guests. In a way, it was strange that we were so worried about the people of the waterfront, for of all of the people we'd met, there had not been an unfriendly one among them.

When we camped within city limits, we could not build a fire. Breakfast we could do without, but the day just didn't seem to start out right without a cup of tea. Sammy and I staggered into town early the next morning. Much to our pleasure, we found a small local restaurant and had a hearty breakfast. Our day started out well and only got better. We raced down river all day. We met many barges and encountered a few wing dams, but had no problems save one. A Coast Guard cutter was coming up the channel. We had taken a short cut and were not in the channel. It blasted its horn at us several times. Sammy and I waved thinking they were just being friendly. The Coast Guard cutter again blasted its horn, and again we waved. For a third time the horn echoed across the river, and we responded with a wave—shortly thereafter we dropped over a wing dam hidden by the high water. Fortunately, it was a small dam, and we swept over it with ease.

"I'm not so sure the crew on that Coast Guard cutter was just being friendly," I told Sammy. "I think they were trying to warn us about the dam we were coming up on."

"They must think we're nuts!" said Sammy.

That evening I was restless. I slowly shuffled through the cool sand in my bare feet until darkness separated me from our camp. Behind me I could see Eureka outlined in the orange glow of the fire and Sammy, squatted like some ancient cave man next to the blaze. Slowly I worked my way up on a bluff. The air was calm and the half-mile wide river lay luminous and silvery before me. From my treeless hill, I could clearly see the Big Dipper and a vast twinkling mass of stars. The moon was no more than a mere sliver in the sky; its bright beams danced across my warm cup of tea. The sound of the river lapping against the shore rose to my ears, its steady pulse accented by the chirp of crickets and the croak of frogs. I sipped my tea and took several breaths of the clean, cool night air. Just then everything about the sort of life Sammy and I had been living seemed very beautiful and perfect. I wished I could preserve that moment forever, but my mind refused to stand still. I thought of my folks and how they must have worried, and for a moment I recalled the threat of those violent Hudson Bay storms. I remembered the exhausting feeling of working all day and moving less than ten miles during the trek through the interior of Canada, the helpless feeling of being without food, the discomfort of those hot days on the Red River, and more recently rainy days that stretched on forever. I did something I hadn't done for a long time. I knelt and prayed, and perhaps with more real meaning in that sanctuary of natural beauty than in a church of stained glass and polished brick. All I could utter was, "My God, we're really going to make it. Praise your holy and merciful name." I wept.

It seemed Sammy and I weren't the only ones headed south, for the sighting of V-formations of ducks had become a daily scene. As we got nearer to New Orleans, there was a lot of southbound traffic on the river other than *Little Eric*. Just north of Baton Rouge a Coast Guard cutter came plowing through the water toward us, until they were so close we were sure we were about to be rammed. Then a sailor appeared on the lower deck and motioned us to come alongside.

"Oh boy," I said to Sammy, "looks like we're going to get some kind of lecture."

When we were tied securely alongside the brightly painted green and white tug, the sailor told us we were wanted in the pilothouse. There we were greeted not by a lecture, but with handshakes and a smile. "Heard you boys were coming down-river," said the man apparently in charge. "You've already taken a lot of guff from this river," he continued, "but we feel you may be headed for some problems up ahead. You're coming to an outflow, a manmade river that diverts the floodwaters from New Orleans. It sort of kills two birds with one stone. It keeps another river deep enough for barges to navigate and prevents New Orleans from flooding. Right now the water's so high, we aren't sure you can get past the outflow without being drawn in, so thought we'd give you a lift." After a pleasant visit, and a safe transport past the outflow, Sammy and I were underway again.

There are few places for larger boats or yachts to refuel between St. Louis and New Orleans. Sammy and I came upon a houseboat whose occupants were learning that the hard way. They thought they had enough fuel to reach Baton Rouge, but not enough to be hunting about for a place to refuel. They asked us to get to the city first, find the fuel stop, and come lead them to it. So, as they drifted along as slowly as possible, Sammy and I headed for Baton Rouge at full throttle. We were glad to be the ones helping someone else out for a change. We located Red's Boat Store, the fuel stop they were looking for; then returned to mid-stream just in time to intercept the house-boat drifters. Together we headed for shore and the spot where both the houseboat and *Little Eric* would be tied for the night. Sammy and I checked in with Vern again, as he was trying to keep close track of us as we neared New Orleans.

From Baton Rouge south, we were to have another new experience, for oceangoing vessels venture as far upstream as the many wharfs of Baton Rouge. The first ship we met was a long black and white ship flying the Japanese flag. It moved swiftly and silently toward us. By now Sammy and I were well acquainted with barges and what they did to the river, but we had no idea what to expect from a ship. We decided to pull into shore and see what effect the ship's passing had on the river. That was the worst move Sammy and I had made in a long time. The bow of the mighty ship rolled up a furrow of water; from the stern rose a wake that started out as a wide, smoothly domed wave, but as those waves neared the shore and shallow water, they narrowed, grew steep, and started to roll noisily like mighty breakers.

Realizing what was coming, Sammy and I jumped from the canoe and tried pulling it far up on shore, but we were too late. The breakers foamed around us splattering us and our gear with a solid coat of mud and water. Dripping wet and covered with mud, Sammy and I stood there looking at each other. Wiping the gunk from my mustache, I said, "Sammy, I think we should meet the next ship in the deep water."

Smiling as if the idea hadn't already been in his mind, he said, "Hey, good idea."

We soon met our next ship, a big American freighter. As we headed toward it, Sammy raised his paddle in the air and shouted, "Ramming speed!" His threat seemed to have little effect on the course of the ship. We met the ship in deep water but stayed a respectable distance away from it to avoid any undertow it may have created. Once the ship glided past us, we headed directly for the big waves created by its massive bulk. We rolled up one side of them and down the other as gently as a mother rocking her baby. *Little Eric* never once bounced out of the water, and with our newly acquired knowledge, we no longer feared meeting the big ships. Like any other form of river traffic, we simply and respectfully shared the river with them.

Our final camp was on a grassy field just north of New Orleans. In an almost symbolic gesture, one of the elastic bands that supported Eureka on its metal frame broke as we put up the tent. Holding one end of the broken strand in his hand Sammy said, "Looks like Eureka is ready to stop traveling too."

We both knew this was our final campsite, but somehow it seemed unreal. It was hard to believe that tomorrow would be the last day of our long journey.

Even our last few miles on the Mississippi would not pass uneventfully. We met ship after ship, some going north, some going south. Yachts, tugs, and ferries cut across the river in every direction. We bounced from one wave to another, unable to hit even half of them at the proper angle as they came at us from all directions at once. The thought of having come this far and then sinking crossed my mind as we got caught in the crossfire of wakes between two large ships. People on the yachts and tugs looked at us like we were out of our minds canoeing through such a high-traffic port area. There were points when Sammy and I likely would have agreed with them, but for the most part, we held our heads high, went about our business, and claimed our right to be on the river.

We powered our way under the shadow of the Huey Long Bridge, and like the end of the rainbow, our landing point was in sight: Jackson Park, New Orleans, Louisiana. Then the seemingly inevitable happened. The pin sheered in our trusty little kicker. Scanning the shoreline, we saw only a solid line of ships and piers with no place to land. We had changed pins on the water before, but to do so just then would have been like walking across an intersection blindfolded. So we did the next best thing. We stripped to our waists and started paddling. Stroke by stroke the final mile of an estimated 5,200 miles of canoeing came to an end, fittingly with sweat and hard toil, for it was those elements and the blessings of God that had carried us through. The Schield Expedition was over. We had canoed from the northern shores of Hudson Bay to the delta of the Mississippi River where it flows into the Gulf of Mexico. We'd quite literally traversed most of North America by canoe.

When the crowd of spectators and the press that had gathered to witness our arrival in New Orleans finally started to dissipate, for a few minutes I sat alone on the shoreline where we'd pulled *Little Eric* up. In silence I watched the river traffic and the swollen waters of the Mississippi as they raced toward the gulf. Like a marathon runner that had finally crossed the finish line, I felt both exhausted and a deep down in your soul type of elation. I reached up and took the medallion, which had been given to me by my friends five months earlier, from around my neck. I held it in my hand and read the inscription, "With you all the way: Gott Segne Euch—God bless you." A wry smile crossed my face, and I simply looked up and said, "Thank you." Indeed I was blessed. We had made it.

Barry reflects on the past 5,200 miles.

Epilogue

About three years after the expedition's conclusion, some neighbors from my hometown of Grand Rapids, Minnesota, visited Churchill. They hired a guide to take them across the Churchill River to see the historic remnants of Fort Churchill. During their casual conversation with the guide, they mentioned they were from the United States. The guide said, "I know someone from the States—do you know Barry Lane?" Their guide was Jimmy Spence! He sent his greetings and that was the last I ever heard from any of my Arctic or Cree travel companions other than Sammy. By now it is likely they have all passed away.

My father, Rex Lane, is now in his nineties. We don't canoe together anymore, but in the summer of 2008, we managed nearly daily fishing outings on his pontoon boat, and on hot summer days, we still reminisce about some of the miserable conditions we suffered through together on the Red River.

I reconnected with young Tom Dean once after the trip. He was invited to Minneapolis to be part of a film documentary about the Schield Canoe Expedition that was narrated by noted television newscaster, Dave Moore. I lost contact with the Deans after the documentary was completed.

Sammy returned to Canada. He eventually discovered a real love relationship and got married and had a family. We remained friends and stayed in contact until his untimely death in the 1980s.

Vern moved nearly everything from the expedition into his museum in Waverly, Iowa, and enjoyed telling the story about the expedition he'd sponsored to anyone that would listen. When I returned to Gustavus Adolphus College, the term after the canoe trip ended, Vern kept his word and paid for one semester's worth of tuition—that was the only compensation I received for leading the expedition. Vern and I visited on occasion and exchanged Christmas cards until both he and his wife, Marjorie, passed away in the early 1990s.

There are a thousand other remembrances, experiences, and pictures permanently engrained in my heart, mind, and spirit that were not included in this written account. You met many of my traveling companions, ardent supporters, and contacts made during my travels, but not all. Many that have gone unnamed in this story touched my life in a significant way, and I will forever be grateful to them for their help, encouragement, and the kindness they showed when our paths crossed.

The day I returned to my home town of Grand Rapids, Minnesota, I found out that my dog, Nugget, had been critically ill for some time. I immediately went to her side. As soon as she saw me, she started to tremble with excitement and struggled to sit up. I bent down; she laid her head in my right hand, closed her eyes, and quietly died. It was as if she'd determined to hang on just long enough for me to return. It was quite a gut wrenching homecoming.

In 1973 a college colleague and I, accompanied by a pack burro and dog, retraced on foot the overland routes of the pioneer wagon trains from Mexico to Minnesota—another expedition story yet to be written! I graduated from Gustavus Adolphus College with majors in both biology and speech. Eventually I went on to complete a doctoral degree in leadership studies from Regent University and currently serve as vice president for a multi-campus college in Minnesota.

I am a man that is neither outwardly demonstrative nor secretive about my faith. My belief in Jesus Christ as my personal Lord and Savior is simply a part of who I am. I hope that was honestly and practically reflected in this book; the journey I completed was truly both a real-life adventure and an adventure of faith. The scriptures identified at the beginning of each chapter became very real to me as I lived through the experiences I shared. I believe our fast-paced lives and the independence and individuality afforded us by modern conveniences often distance us from the presence of our heavenly Father and the intimate relationship He desires to have with us. While living in the most primitive of conditions, often questioning our safety or where our next meal would come from, I found a nearness to the Lord that shaped my life and faith forever. I have known hunger and He fed me; I have known fear and He gave me peace, and when I lacked the skill or knowledge to meet the challenges of the situations I found myself in He provided me with His mercy, protection, and hope.

My life has forever been blessed by the unique experience I had during the five months of the Schield Canoe Expedition. As you face your own life journey, with its unique challenges and experiences, may you too turn to Jesus in faith and feel his nearness, comfort, and hope.

–Dr. Barry L. Lane

e|LIVE

listen|imagine|view|experience

AUDIO BOOK DOWNLOAD INCLUDED WITH THIS BOOK!

In your hands you hold a complete digital entertainment package. Besides purchasing the paper version of this book, this book includes a free download of the audio version of this book. Simply use the code listed below when visiting our website. Once downloaded to your computer, you can listen to the book through your computer's speakers, burn it to an audio CD or save the file to your portable music device (such as Apple's popular iPod) and listen on the go!

How to get your free audio book digital download:

1. Visit www.tatepublishing.com and click on the e|LIVE logo on the home page.
2. Enter the following coupon code:
   1341-7c2c-2104-91bd-d6e0-e8d8-ac7e-360f
3. Download the audio book from your e|LIVE digital locker and begin enjoying your new digital entertainment package today!